Jim Thorpe Never Slept Here

And Other Stories From A Mauch Chunk, Pennsylvania Boyhood

PENNSYLVANIA HERITAGE BOOKS
An Imprint of University of Scranton Press
Scranton and London

An imprint in honor of Joseph P. McKerns (1950-2004)
Of Shenandoah and Mahanoy City
Grandson of Irish and Polish immigrants who worked the
Railroads and coal mines of Pennsylvania
Champion of those working men and women
Who have always been Pennsylvania's greatest heritage

Jim Thorpe Never Slept Here

And Other Stories From A Mauch Chunk,
Pennsylvania Boyhood

Richard Benyo

PENNSYLVANIA HERITAGE BOOKS
An Imprint of
University of Scranton Press
Scranton and London

© 2008 University of Scranton Press
All rights reserved

Library of Congress Cataloging-in-Publication Data

Benyo, Richard.
Jim Thorpe never slept here : and other stories from a Mauch Chunk, Pennsylvania
boyhood / Richard Benyo.
p. cm.
Includes bibliographical references and index.
ISBN 978-1-58966-166-0 (pbk. : alk. paper)

1. Benyo, Richard — Childhood and youth. 2. Mauch Chunk (Pa.)--Biography.
3. Jim Thorpe (Pa.) — Biography. 4. Boys — Pennsylvania — Mauch Chunk — Biography. 5. Boys — Pennsylvania — Jim Thorpe — Biography. 6. Mauch Chunk
(Pa.) — Social life and customs — 20th century. 7. Jim Thorpe (Pa.) — Social life and
customs — 20th century. I. Title.

F159.M4B46 2008

974.8'26 — dc22

[B]

2008002167

Distribution:
University of Scranton Press
Chicago Distribution Center
11030 S. Langley
Chicago, IL 60628

PRINTED IN THE UNITED STATES OF AMERICA

To the members of the South Street Gang — those extinct and extant.

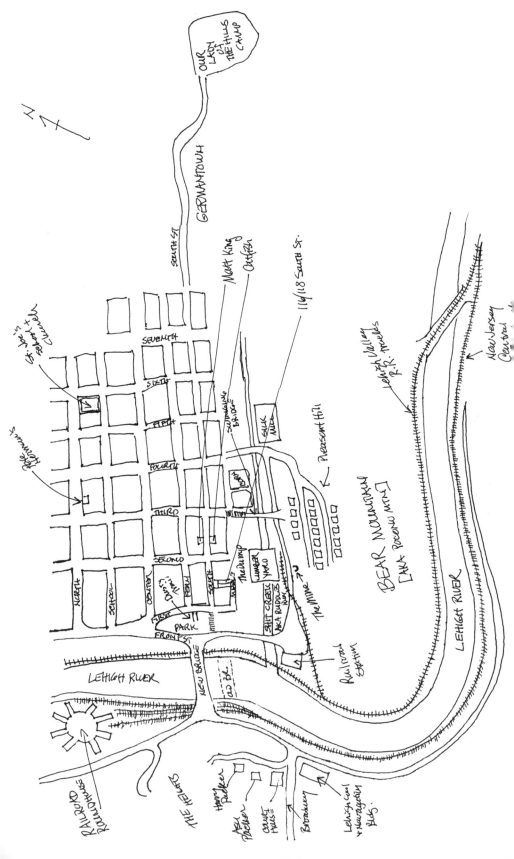

Disclaimer

Because this is a book of stories about a boy's life in the '40s and '50s of postwar America, I have used a great number of brand names — most iconic, others more obscure — to help conjure up the true flavor and feel of that time and place.

In these pages, you'll find passing references to food, candy, and liquid refreshments (Manwich, Wrigley's Spearmint Gum, Kool-Aid, Mary Janes, Bazooka Bubble Gum, B-B-Bats, Bit-O-Honey, Dots, Tastykakes, Raisinettes, Wheaties, RC Cola, and Hershey bars), comic-book makers (Marvel, DC, and Dell), cartoon, comic-strip, and comic-book characters (Beetle Bailey, Bozo, Bugs Bunny, Casper, Batman, Superman, Aquaman, Wonder Woman, Donald Duck, Daffy Duck, Scrooge McDuck, Little Lulu, Popeye, Porky Pig, Peanuts, The Flash, The Lone Ranger, The Whistler, The Fantastic Four, Captain America, Captain Marvel, The Justice League of America, The Justice Society of America, and Dale Evans, Queen of the West), books, magazines, movies, and TV shows (*The Red Badge of Courage*, *The Little Engine That Could*, *Little Black Sambo*, and *Lord of the Flies*; *National Enquirer*, *American Rifleman*, and *Playboy*; *Marathon Man*, *The Molly Maguires*, and *Silence of the Lambs*; *The Mickey Mouse Club*, *Wild Kingdom*, *The Adventures of Ozzie and Harriet*, and *Welcome Back, Kotter*), kids' toys and such (Radio Flyer, Frisbee, Play-Doh, Silly Putty, Topps trading cards, Crayola crayons, and Magic Markers), various companies (Chevy, GE, Publishers Clearing House, Samsonite, Grosset & Dunlop, Schlage, and Xerox), and even Mr. Clean.

A few of these (such as Xerox, Magic Markers, *Silence of the Lambs*, and *Welcome Back, Kotter*) could only be referred to anachronistically, of course, but even then my point was to convey the incidents and emotions as clearly as possible.

It should go without saying that I have no intention of diluting the value or challenging the ownership of these or any other trademarked or copyright-protected properties. (I'm told that some company even owns the rights to the name of Jim Thorpe — and Marilyn Monroe, and James Dean, and Jesse Owens, and a hundred others.) Well, I don't want to get crosswise with anybody.

So, I acknowledge these and all registered trademarks and copyrights to be those of their owners. I only borrowed them, okay?

Contents

Geopolitics

The former Speaker of the House "Tip" O'Neil once said, "All politics are local." If he meant that all politics are based on geography, I wholeheartedly agree. (But then, who studies geography these days? What student today knows the difference between an isthmus and a peninsula when Ivy League grads can't even find the good old USA on a map of the world?) But anyway, this axiom — that geography dictates politics — is understood by even the least urbane first grader who lives in a place where a river runs through it. Or a railroad bisects it. Or a bridge spans it. Or mountains hem it in and, all the while, his mother forbids him to explore it.

We grew up in a mountain-enfolded river valley, with railroads on both sides of the river and a single rickety bridge — connecting the two hardscrabble boroughs of East Mauch Chunk and Mauch Chunk, Carbon County, in central-eastern Pennsylvania, roughly halfway between Wilkes-Barre/Scranton and Philadelphia. *Machk Tschunk* was Leni Lenape Indian for *Bear Mountain*, a millennially worn-down mountain that supposedly resembled a sleeping bear, although most of us living in its shadow and peering up at it on a daily basis couldn't see that slumbering bruin. Perhaps we needed to move farther away in order to put a sharper edge to our imaginations.

The Lehigh River flowed around the rounded-head end of Bear Mountain, while East Mauch Chunk (originally known as *The Kettle*, and laid out on Lehigh Coal & Navigation Company land) spread out gently on an ancient alluvial fan on the northwest side of the mountain. Mauch Chunk, the county seat, was more precariously situated on the other side of the river — half of it (*Downtown,* i.e. Broadway and its arteries) scrunched between the close-packed, tired old Appalachian Mountains, and the other half (*The Heights*) perched atop a plateau coming off the side of Mount Pisgah, which squeezed Broadway from the north.

Mauch Chunk had been, at the turn of the twentieth century, the home of a dozen millionaires. Most prominent of them was Asa Packer, Lehigh Valley Railroad tycoon and founder of Lehigh University. His Victorian Italianate mansion perched on the lowest thrust of Mount Pisgah just above the county courthouse.

That's the same courthouse where, back in 1879, the good citizens of the county tried the Molly Maguires, a band of Irish "terrorists" who had the audacity to demand a living wage in exchange for crawling down into the earth six days a week to harvest anthracite coal so Philadelphia and New York City could heat their homes — and so Asa Packer could get rich sending the coal to market on his canal barges and his railroad. Several Molly Maguires, after being tried in the courthouse, were hanged in the jail, about a half-mile up Broadway. Hollywood shot a movie, *The Molly Maguires*, in 1968 and used Mauch Chunk as the "big city" to which the miners traveled for a day on the town. They hanged Sean Connery at the jailhouse after Richard Harris ratted on him. (The two stars drank together into the wee hours at Weiksner's Bar across from the courthouse when they were finished with their day's work, acting.)

Most of the local fortunes were made by entrepreneurs mining and shipping coal to market, either by rail or canal barge, both of which departed downhill from Mauch Chunk. Mauch Chunk itself escaped by a mile or two the environmental devastation of hard-coal strip mining.

By the time I came along in 1946, the area was in the grip of the coal-miner blues resulting from the demise of King Coal in the wake of home-heating alternatives such as heating oil and electricity (ironically, generated by burning coal). There were still some mines operating in Coaldale and Lansford "up the road" — as we referred to the chain of working coal-mining towns. And most people in Mauch Chunk and East Mauch Chunk still heated their homes with coal and tried to keep some pride in their history and to keep the profession going. They hung placards in their windows saying

"We Heat With Coal" much as they'd hung single-star banners in their windows during World War II, declaring that a serviceman from their family was fighting the good fight. But even then, the writing (that coal wasn't the way to go) was on the wall right next to the placard. Many of the male heads-of-households commuted, dozens of miles, to work in manufacturing jobs having nothing to do with coal.

Anchored to the hillside and brooding above the Asa Packer Mansion sat his son's, made of stone, the Harry Packer Mansion. For most of the years of my youth it was deserted, and we considered it haunted. It was so good at defining haunted, in fact, that when Walt Disney built Disney World in Florida, his designers used the Harry Packer Mansion as the model for the Haunted Mansion. (Most of the other millionaire mansions — and the millionaires who went with them — were long gone.)

Our two tired little towns, together sporting a population of roughly five thousand — with the emphasis on *rough* — was, like much of the coal region, a hotbed of prejudice, but prejudice of a very particular white-person variety, based almost entirely on nationality. For example, there was the dual Catholic prejudice. The Immaculate Conception Catholic Parish was located on Broadway (just above the jailhouse) in Mauch Chunk proper; it was the Irish-Catholic Catholic church. On Sixth and North streets in East Mauch Chunk was St. Joseph's (St. Joe's), the German-Catholic Catholic church.

Since there were quite a few Slovaks living in East Mauch Chunk, they went to the German-Catholic church, although they were considered a lower species of Catholics by the Germans. Similarly, although they were nominally of the same religion (as members of the Roman Catholic Church, they shared the same pope), an Irish-Catholic marrying a German-Catholic was, in our town, considered a mixed marriage. God forbid an Irish-Catholic should marry a Lutheran! Or a Presbyterian kid play with a German-Catholic!

The river was the ultimate dividing line on just about every topic as, at least until 1954, these were two very separate and distinct towns. But the exceptions to the prejudice rules also involved the river. For instance, not everyone in East Mauch Chunk was German or Slovak. We had a sprinkling of Irish; there were some Italians, some Jews, and even an Arab family. But because they lived on the east side of the river, they were *our* Irish, *our* Italians, *our* Jews, and *our* Arabs. They were okay — in spite of the occasional evidence that some of their loyalties leapt the river (except for the Arabs, for there were no fellow Arabs in Mauch Chunk). They were all stuck being East Chunkers just like the rest of us.

We German and Slovak-Catholics were most prejudiced against the Irish across the river, and they against us.

It was all politics, and it was all in the curves and wrinkles of the land. It was so deep-seated, and was made so enormous by legend, that we kids from the East Side seldom crossed the bridge unless accompanied by adults, who could ostensibly protect us from being beaten, killed, dismembered, and possibly eaten by the merciless and obviously muddle-headed Irish. The one exception was Saturday afternoon, when every kid in town called a truce and went to the town's one movie house — the old opera house on Broadway — for the cartoons, cliffhanger serial, and a double feature, all for 13 cents.

After dark, it was unthinkable to cross the bridge alone, although in typical kid fashion, we did occasionally egg each other into creeping across to the other side, since there were no homes and therefore no enemies precisely at the far side of the bridge, just a cliff face atop which The Heights rested. (Mauch Chunk proper lay around a curve to the left.) On summer evenings, after supper (our families always called the evening meal *supper*, not *dinner*; *dinner*, to us, was the noon meal), we'd gather at the park just above our side of the bridge, above where River Street emptied onto the bridge. And we'd imagine what the Irish-Catholics would do to us if they ever caught us on their side of the river after dark. That was their geography over there. And we'd bravely run down a litany of the worst things we could think of that we'd do to them if any of them ventured onto *our* side of the bridge. We talked real big among ourselves. Talk costs nothing.

We weren't yet well-read enough or with-it enough to know to call them *Micks*. But we knew what they called us because we used the words ourselves. Most of us were *Hunkies* — low-caste Slovaks whose families had come over after the First World War (*The Great War*, according to our antique nun teachers), whose grandparents could barely speak English, whose grandfathers had worked in the mines or on the railroads, and who felt it was a sin against God and the Church to have an only child. Many of the rest were *Heinies, Krauts, Jerries* — Germans, whose grandparents or great-grandparents typically came over before The Great War. (Most of the German grandparents had been raised here and spoke perfectly good American English.)

I was neither Hunky nor Heinie, but rather half of each: a *Hunk o' Heinie*. My mother was German-American and my father Slovak-American, and the only common trait the two families shared was the stereotypical pigheadedness of both nationalities.

Our block on lower South Street was a real United Nations of white people. We had Slovaks whose last names ended in the letter "o": Bronko, Franko, Tomasko. We had our Germans: Otto, Bretz, Mertz. We had our Irish: Gallagher, Carroll, McHugh. And assorted others. But there were no Negroes (the respectful term for African-Americans in those days) in either East Mauch Chunk or Mauch Chunk, and no Asians. (We did get a few Puerto Rican kids from New York City or New Jersey in the summer as a result of the Fresh Air Kids Program, although many of them claimed to be Spanish.)

When hanging around the railroad station to watch the trains drop off and pick up passengers, we'd occasionally see a nattily attired train porter or conductor — his exotic darkness set off by his polished brass buttons. Being an avid fan of *Amos 'n' Andy*, I once asked an older kid why no Negroes lived in East Mauch Chunk. It being a low-self-esteem day in East Mauch Chunk, the kid considered that no self-respecting Negro would want to.

We lived in the middle of the block in the uphill side of a duplex — or as we called it, a *double house*. The Bretz family lived on the other side of the dividing wall. The Henritzys, Lewie and Ellie, an older couple, lived in the house next to us on the uphill side. The Henritzys used to rent our house, and when the owners decided to sell it, the Henritzys simply moved next door. My parents always felt Lewie and Ellie held a grudge because my parents bought their house out from under them and had, in essence, *evicted* them. I never saw it that way, but then my parents always had a peculiar way of interpreting what other people thought and a twisted way of explaining why neighbors did what they did.

Behind our house, straddling the back yards of 116 and 118 South Street, was a two-hole outhouse, again with a dividing wall, one side for us and the other side for the Bretzes, with a common ditch underneath. (There was no central sewage at that time.) Mr. Bretz was something of a sour old fellow and, at times, while I sat warming the wooden toilet seat on our side of the outhouse, he'd bring out a rock and throw it down into the ditch, apparently trying to splash crap up onto my lily-white butt. (It was nothing personal, though; he'd do it for any of us Benyos.) With Lewie and Ellie on one side, and Mr. and Mrs. Bretz on the other, we were surrounded by perceived enemies; it was all geography.

The backyards sloped down to what was officially known as Maple Street, which ended behind the Henritzys' back yard. The whole back end of east South Street at that point dropped off precipitously toward Ruddle's Run, a creek that ran through the valley behind our houses and the base of Bear Mountain. Everyone whose property backed onto what we called *The Dump* used the hillside as a common dumping ground for garbage — not unlike those ancient civilizations that delight archeologists, although their delight in South Street's empty tuna cans and wine jugs might be stretching scientific enthusiasms. There was no town-wide garbage pickup at that time. Those civilizing factors (central sewage, garbage pickup) were waiting until the mid-'50s, and beyond, to raise us up from our primitive habits and habitat.

In the valley below The Dump, the lumberyard straddled Ruddle's Run — a.k.a. *The Shit Creek*. Everyone in the vicinity of Ruddle's Run referred to it as The Shit Creek (pronounced "crick") because the silk mill at the upper end of the valley dumped its liquid refuse into it, and a goodly number of houses along the creek's sides ran pipes from their indoor plumbing directly into it. It all then ran into the Lehigh River, where we sometimes swam in the summer. From the remove of fifty years, it sounds like a particularly grim scene from Dickens.

On the opposite side of the valley was Bear Mountain. The mini-community scabbed onto the lower side of Bear Mountain was named Pleasant Hill. At one time Pleasant Hill was home to many, many Slovak miners and their families. From our backyard, looking across the valley, we could see the house on Pleasant Hill where our father had been born in a second-story bedroom.

When we kids were underfoot and were shooed outside to play, we'd typically head for one of two venues: The Dusty Trail or The Dump. No video games or Internet for us. No virtual reality, either; just plain old, everyday, good-and-dirty reality.

The Dusty Trail was a scuffed bit of path cut through the underbrush at the high side of the park down the street. The park was bordered by First Street on the top and River Street on the bottom. The Dusty Trail was like a scab a kid constantly picks at so that it never heals. The rest of that side of the park was walled by shrubs — except for the entrance we had cut through by dragging our sneakers, creating a dust cloud like the cowboys riding their horses across a Western landscape in the Saturday afternoon movies. We picked that spot on which to make our entrance because it led straight as an arrow to the tallest tree in the park, which we were regularly inclined to climb. When our mother wanted to find me or my brother, she'd ask one of the neighbor ladies, and the answer would frequently be, "Oh, yeah. I saw them about an hour ago, down The Dusty."

The Dump, as I've told you, was the garbage dump behind our houses where we had cut a trail through the garbage, angled like a long downhill skiing traverse, from our backyard down to the upper end of the lumberyard where a plank crossed over the Shit Creek. Several other trails cut off to other paths that led to places like Catfish Gavornik's house on the second block of South Street. The upper reaches of the paths worked their way through tin cans, empty wine jugs, dead mattresses, decomposing yard clippings, and the like, but the trash didn't extend all the way down the bank and was soon left behind.

After dark, we avoided The Dump. Full-grown adult males who'd fought the Jerries and Japs during World War II avoided The Dump after dark, too, once the red eyes of the dump rats began to blink on. The Dump, like any dump (more recently called *landfills*), was a breeding ground for rats. The only thing that kept them from overrunning the neighborhood, and moving lock, stock, and stiletto tails into our homes, was the fact that Mr. Mertz raised and trained an army of cats to do battle with the rats on a daily basis. Our street was one of the only places in America where adult males actually liked and respected cats.

The rats were a good excuse for kids to get BB guns for birthdays and Christmas. There was no such thing as being too young to own your own BB gun. The BBs seldom did any real damage to the rats, but getting hit did sting their pride enough to make them leery about advancing too far up our backyards.

"Don't play down at The Dump!" Dorothy, my mother, would always warn us.

That one was right up there with such admonitions as:

"Don't ever put money in your mouth; you don't know where it's been!"

"Don't bite your fingernails; they'll clump together in your stomach and you'll bleed to death!"

"Don't play with so-and-so; you'll get head lice and we'll have to shave you bald!"

Naturally, every chance we got we'd bite on our coins like movie pirates to see if they were gold, we'd gnaw our fingernails mercilessly, and we'd play with so-and-so — usually at The Dump.

We figured we were pretty safe from the rats during the daylight hours. It was around sundown when it became dangerous to be near The Dump. The rats were big and they were bad and they were bold. And they were generally nocturnal. When we occasionally did encounter a rat during the day, it wouldn't skitter away to safety like a citified cockroach. It stood its ground and dared us to do something about it.

As I've said, the first line of defense against the dreaded rats was Mr. Mertz's motley army of tomcats. In those days, America was a dog country. Cats were loathed and the object of many a cruel aggression. "They're sneaky and dirty," our mother would say, referring to Mr. Mertz's cats — thereby implying that it was true of all cats. (Heck, the same description could have been applied to at least half of my classmates.)

Of course Mr. Mertz's cats were sneaky and dirty. *That* was their *job*. Their job was to sneak around The Dump and kill enough of the big, belligerent rats to keep them from becoming bold enough that they'd come up through the backyards in waves to attack us in our beds! *Of course* Mr. Mertz's cats were sneaky. And *dirty*, too. We got just as dirty as they did when we hung around The Dump all day.

The poor cats were dirty and tattered because all day and night they roamed The Dump looking to get into fights with rats, who were genetically inclined to oblige. There wasn't one tomcat among the South Street Defender Corps that wasn't festooned with scars from claw-to-claw and tooth-to-tooth combat with those rats. Pieces of ears were missing, one of the orange cats had lost an eye, patches of fur the size of a man's wallet were gone, and there were scars along their flanks and everywhere else, too. After a particularly nasty battle, the cats who were involved limped around for the next several days and licked their wounds under Mr. Mertz's back porch until they were strong enough to rejoin the endless fray.

Occasionally when we were playing down at The Dump, we'd come across one of Mr. Mertz's cats who'd taken some pretty serious hits. Usually, the cat was too weak to put up much of a fight against us picking it up. We'd gently carry the limp cat up through Mr. Mertz's backyard and knock on his back door and run, leaving the cat lying by the door. All the kids were afraid of Mr. Mertz because he had a serious limp (like the lurch of Frankenstein's monster in the movies) but was built like a pulling guard, and he and his sickly wife had a tendency to keep to themselves.

Mr. Mertz got old, and he cut back on the number of cats he kept. When his wife died, he took all of her prescription medicines (and there were shopping bags full of them) and threw them in The Dump. By then we were old enough to realize that the stuff in the medicine bottles was dangerous. We took the bags home to be properly disposed of so that none of the dumb little kids in the neighborhood would find them and think it was candy.

But Dorothy's response wasn't, "Good job, boys!" It was: "I thought I told you to never play at The Dump!" *Whack!* "Just you wait until your father gets home! He'll beat The Dump out of you!" And, true to Dorothy's promise, he did.

Gradually, after borough-wide garbage pickup was initiated, The Dump began to heal as the neighbors dumped the coal ashes from their stokers, eventually covering up the trash and garbage. Of course, we'd occasionally have to rush down to The Dump with the garden hose when someone dumped a load of ashes that hadn't quite cooled. As the ashes gradually covered The Dump, the rat population declined.

The valley, above which The Dump squatted on the western lip, served as a sort of megaphone for the regular sound of train whistles from the two rail lines (The New Jersey Central and the Lehigh Valley) that ran along the river between the two towns. On a summer night, the whistles would reverberate up the valley and soothe us to sleep. Today it's a too-seldom-heard sound that can still be soothing for the warm memories it stirs.

The presence of two railroads, served first by coal-burning steam locomotives and later by diesel engines, had a pretty devastating effect on the trees on both sides of the river — those few trees that were left from the wholesale cutting that went on in the 1800s and early 1900s as barges were built to transport coal down the canal along the Lehigh River to Easton and on to Philadelphia, and then were dismantled in the City of Brotherly Love and turned into houses. But, from an environmental standpoint, things in the town gradually improved. The train traffic diminished and the trees grew back, thicker than ever. Central sewage was put in; the outhouses were torn down and the pits filled in. Garbage was collected on a garbage truck instead of collecting behind houses. The old rickety bridge was replaced by one made of concrete so that when you walked across it you no longer had to take a giant step over missing planks to avoid falling into the angry river far below.

There was still very little industry, and the men, who had previously worked the coal mines or the railroads, commuted in car pools to Hazleton or to jobs at the Palmerton Zinc Smelting Plant or the Bethlehem Steel Company. Some of the geographically-induced animosity between the two towns was dissipated in 1954 when the two sides voted to combine into one town and take the name of the famed (and disgraced) American Indian athlete Jim Thorpe. But that's a whole 'nother story.

Looking back at East Mauch Chunk from fifty years and three thousand miles away, I see it has for me its own unique nostalgic patina. It was at once a terrific place to be a kid and a frustrating place to be a teenager. And I think you'll agree, as I share some of my memories, that there are a lot of much-less-interesting places I could have come from.

Hard-Boiled Mother

There are those who contend that the breath and texture of our lives are molded like so much Play-Doh by the alignment of the stars and planets at the moment of birth. It's ideas like this that differentiate us from the lesser animals, whose time is more constructively spent collecting nuts against the winter or scratching at fleas.

It seems unlikely to me that two people born on the same day are going to be any more similar than two people born on different days who have other factors in common, such as genes, religious upbringing (or lack of same), geographical proximity, parents, or siblings. There are, of course, exceptions. Emil Zatopek and his wife Dana were born on the very same day (September 19, 1922) in Czechoslovakia, and both went on to win Olympic gold medals in track and field at the 1952 Olympic Games.

I think there are better uses for the stars and planets. They are wonderful to walk under, wonderful to contemplate, wonderful as a setting for science fiction novels, wonderful anchors for navigation, and wonderfully plentiful.

There are others, however, who contend that the breath and texture of our lives are fashioned by the intricate and lovely helix of genes and chromosomes that form when two human beings toss together their ancestries on the roulette wheel of sex (and hence, procreation). Incidentally, did you know that the sperm is the smallest cell in the male body and that the ovum is the largest cell in the female body? It's true. And when the two come together, there is a great battle waged between dominant and recessive genes — in which the dominant aren't always dominant.

I'm not very popular with acquaintances who are of the Nurture persuasion. *Their* feeling, of course, is that nurturing, good or bad, makes us what we are. Were that so, I think siblings would be much more alike than they usually are, even taking into consideration the effects of birth order and what I think of as *regressive parenting*—i.e., less hands-on parenting for each successive child.

I subscribe to the theory that Nature, the roulette wheel of the genes, has much more to do with who a person is than nurturing ever does. Not that nurturing is unimportant, but merely that it is recessive to the dominance of genetics. I think the roulette-spin combination of dominant and recessive traits also accounts for the physical differences in children of the same parents. The kids in a family aren't all clones, as they would be were the dominant genes always to come out on top. I hold dearly to this theory even in the face of the fact that, before I was born, my genetic prospects were rather bleak.

Both my parents — Andrew "Shorty" Benyo and Dorothy "Dot" Herman — so thoroughly considered themselves to be the black sheep of their respective families that they actually prided themselves on their blackness. So let's see now . . . black-sheep-gene-carrying sperm approaches and penetrates black-sheep-gene-carrying ovum. If I truly believed in Nature over Nurture, what a truly bleak start that was for this kid!

Makes me want to sprint to the front of the line when time travel is finally perfected, so I can rush back to July 21, 1945, and when the priest inquires of the congregation, "Are there any present who feel this union should not be consecrated?" I can leap to my feet (or is it *hooves*? Do black sheep have hooves?), right there in little, depressed, worn-out, anthracite-coal-shipping East Mauch Chunk, Pennsylvania, and state my case in the most eloquent way possible to prevent that black-sheep union:

"Think of the kids!"

But let's skip back a few years to see how my parents met. During summers, my father worked as a lifeguard at the Memorial Park pool in East Mauch Chunk. As a pre-teen, my mother cast a covetous eye upon this hunk, eight years her senior, and commenced to chase away any other female who attempted to make a move on him. Nature programs on television always show the male chasing away other males from the female of the species. So what gives? Oh, yeah. I forgot. These weren't lions. They were two black sheep.

When World War II reared its ugly head, Shorty Benyo enlisted in the U.S. Army using forged papers to get himself into Officer Candidate School. He had dropped out of the seventh grade to go to work to help support the family when his father died. The story goes that he broke into the school, secured himself the appropriate blank paperwork, and forged himself a graduation certificate. He came out of OCS a second lieutenant and was shipped off to Panama, where he spent the war training infantry recruits, both in combat readiness and in how to combat VD. (It is my understanding that most guys who die in wars die from disease rather than from enemy fire. Judging from the sex talk he eventually gave me, I'm surprised any of our boys survived WWII with their genitals intact.)

As the war wound down, Shorty and Dot plotted their marriage. There were, however, two impediments to their success:

First, Dorothy's parents didn't much care for Shorty. Recall the prejudice of upper-caste Germans against lower-caste Slovaks. So they refused to agree to her marrying him, which meant she had to wait until she was twenty-one. (She waited them out. Remember pigheaded Germans?)

Second, once they were married, they were transferred for a time to a military base in Alabama until Shorty was turned out of the Army along with millions of other suddenly-redundant soldiers. When they returned to East Mauch Chunk, they had nowhere to live while Shorty searched for a life-fulfilling career, so they ended up with Peter and Mary Herman, my mother's parents. (You remember — the parents who didn't like Shorty from the start.)

But he had a foot in the door. That foot was me. I was scheduled to be the first grandkid (black sheep or not) on my mother's side of the family, and according to the way the Germans think, that was something of a big deal. The fact that I turned out to be a male was even more important. I think there was a lot of primogeniture thinking (you know — the first male gets all the goodies) left over from the Old Country.

Let's pick up the story as we approach Easter weekend of 1946. (I like to think of this story as a whole new definition of fertilized eggs.) Dorothy was very, very pregnant — nearly nine months' worth. This was within a few days of being exactly nine months after the wedding. It was Good Friday, 1946.

It was a tradition in East Mauch Chunk among nearly every nationality to make hard-boiled eggs and then decorate them for use in Easter baskets. Some of the nationalities took this art form to extremes, coloring the eggs and then painting designs on them with colored wax. What colored chicken eggs have to do with the resurrection of Jesus from the tomb, I don't really know. Nor can I claim much knowledge of what Easter bunnies have to do with it, unless it has something to do with both rabbits and Catholics breeding frequently.

After Easter, the casually-colored hard-boiled eggs were shelled and soaked for several days in a mixture of red beets, vinegar, pepper, and salt to make pickled eggs — a delicacy showcased in huge pickle jars on the bar of every self-respecting tavern in every coal town in Pennsylvania. Going into Easter, any eggs that had not been boiled up perfectly were shelled and got a head start on being pickled.

My mother sat at the kitchen table in the Herman house with her belly hanging out over the chair while she shelled damaged eggs and ate roughly every other one, as though the little black lamb living for the past 8.9 months in her abdomen had a lust for hard-boiled eggs — or perhaps it was merely the stereotypical hormone-fueled wacko eating habits of a very pregnant woman. Now, this was a long time before hard-boiled eggs were discovered to be like cholesterol hand grenades. She pulled the plug on one egg after the other, sprinkled on some salt, and knocked them back. Years later, as this tale was told and retold, it began to sound like that scene in *Monty Python's Meaning of Life* where the gluttonous restaurant patron is offered "one thin mint," the ingestion of which causes him to explode.

Eventually the eggs were either in Dorothy's belly or soaking in the beets-and-vinegar brine, and she went to bed. But in the middle of the night she began to suffer what she thought was a tremendous stomachache. "I really overdid it with the eggs." Maybe she felt she was being punished by God for deserting her black sheep persona to become a plain old pig. She still had no clue that she was coming to term with the thing growing in her womb. The ache became so bad she woke my father and he drove her to the Palmerton Hospital. "This awful tummyache. Too many eggs. Oh, dear God, get me through this and I'll never be a big fat pig again."

Dorothy Rita Herman Benyo had apparently been given about as much sex education as her black-sheep husband would, some sixteen years later, impart to his first-born son who was, at that very moment, about to pop out without waiting for Easter Sunday. Sure enough, at 11:40 a.m. on April 20, Easter Saturday, *Boom*! I was cast out of my comfortable apartment by Dorothy's ingestion of several too many hard-boiled eggs. Eight pounds and four ounces, twenty-two inches long, blue eyes, and a head like Mr. Clean. As soon as the family saw the blue eyes (my mother had green eyes and my father brown), jokes about the milkman, Cy Barnes, began to circulate. (If only it were true.)

But here's the scary part if you're to believe in any of that birth-date and astrology stuff—a list of other folks born on April 20 (whether forced out of the womb by hard-boiled eggs or other indignities, I dunno):

- Mohammed (570)
- Napoleon (1808)
- Adolph Hitler (1889)
- Harold Lloyd (1894)
- Johnny Tillotson (1939); you remember — the country and (crossover) pop star who sang "Poetry in Motion" and the theme song "Gidget" for the TV show starring Sally Field.

I rest my case against the stars holding too much sway over the way we turn out.

The Cossmen Yeti

There is a theory, propagated by experts who deal with such things, that holds that the further back in life your memories go, the more intelligent you are. Putting such a theory together for one's own amusement is okay, but advertising it to the general public is asking for trouble. You would think that experts who deal with the human subspecies would have enough sense to realize what the news of this otherwise interesting theory was going to spawn. It spawned just what an unbiased observer of the current human condition would expect — competition, one-upmanship, me-firstism, and turbo-charged egotism.

And, as so often happens in these modern times, the New Agers swished to the front and swept away all intelligent, good-natured competition by claiming that they could trace their memories back not only into early childhood, but right on through it and into the womb itself! Buoyed by their unabashed and uniquely smart-alecky intelligence, there is now an all-out race among various cults and species of New Agers to determine just which of them will be first to claim he or she recalls riding his/her father's sperm on its way to fertilize Mom's egg toward creating his/her own wonderful self. Sort of like Slim Pickens riding the H-bomb in *Dr. Strangelove* — but a lot gooier. (Pity the cold isolation and vacuum of those New Agers who came from a test tube. Sue that lab for short-circuiting precious pre-fertilization memories.)

On occasions when this topic rears its enticing head, I whip together the remnants of whatever brain cells I can round up, cull out those still marginally dedicated to memory, squeeze them together as hard as I can, and the memory that oozes out is always the same:

being held as an infant not by my own mother, but by my great-grandparents, my mother's mother's parents, Edward and Frances Cossman. The precise memory trundles in from my pre-four-month-old era and sticks so tenaciously, not because of the usual visual impression we associate with such things, but because my baby butt was just a mass of nerve endings eager to get tactile stimulation from something other than a dirty diaper. That something, in this case, was the sandpaper hands of my giant great-grandparents, the Cossmen Yeti — *Cossmen*, of course, being the plural of Cossman, the specific gender be dipped.

My great-grandparents wouldn't have been offended by my referring to them as Yeti. They were the hugest people I'd ever known to that point in my life. (This is quite a distinction, considering even a mere kid of six years is a giant to a four-month-old.) In calling my great-grandparents huge, I don't mean that they were big fat slobs. They were just plain tall, like amiable giants from mythology.

During a college music course several millennia later, I would become fascinated with Richard Wagner's *Ring* cycle. My favorite characters were Fafner and Fasolt (I believe their last name, too, was Cossman), the two giants who on commission from the chief god Wotan built the palace Valhalla and then got screwed out of their pay by that same Wotan. As our family legend had it, my great-grandparents were in some major way involved in the building of St. Joseph's Church in East Mauch Chunk, only to be screwed out of the money owed them by that same parish. I have no idea if my very German great-grandparents knew about Wagner's *The Ring of the Nibelung* (they were German, after all), but I suspect they were wise enough in the ways of the world to understand that history sometimes repeats itself.

Somewhere I've got a snapshot of these gentle giants sitting on a bench side by side, Edward holding my leaf-eared, splay-legged, diapered little self. As I recall, they appear severe only in their uncertainty as to the camera's intentions. In the photo, Edward (who bore a passing resemblance to FDR) supports my young buns with one massive hand, cradling the rest of me in the crook of his left arm. Uncomfortable with the camera, they were probably only persuaded to pose for the picture with me because I was their first great-grandchild.

If I inherited anything from my great-grandparents, it was their prominent ears — and the resultant responsibility to be a good listener. I don't remember them being big talkers. My own ears were so prominent that when I was a child my father was kind enough to take note of them on occasion: "You look like a taxi going down Fifth Avenue with its doors open." I didn't know he'd been to New York.

I was held up and passed around a lot when I was an infant, as though nobody had ever seen a baby before, probably because I'd managed to beat the rest of my cousins in the birth race. I imagine that I was a mixed blessing, however. After all, I'd been spawned by two people who were, you'll recall, the black sheep of their respective families, so I wasn't exactly all white.

My black-sheep heritage put a special burden on me. Although Dorothy and Shorty would not visit their own families, even though they lived a mere four and six blocks away respectively, when I was old enough to make the trip alone, I was required under pain of the most extreme punishment to visit my grandparents on a regular basis. The first test I would endure when coming in the kitchen door of Mary Herman's house was the third degree on where my parents were, and why they hadn't come to visit, and what they were doing, et cetera, et cetera, et cetera. And in that perverse trap from which there is no escape, if I stayed at my grandparents too long after being sent there, I'd get myself punished back at home. Shorty's logic: "What? Your own house isn't good enough for you?" Then I'd have the opportunity to undergo *their* third degree with questions about who was at Peter and Mary Herman's house, and what they'd had to eat, and what they'd said, and on, and on, and on.

I do recall enjoying very much our infrequent visits to my *great-*grandparents' house (you remember — the Cossmen Yeti) on Tenth Street. They had a goldfish pond into which I could stare for hours at a time, watching the constant circling and darting of the fish among the lily pads. They also had a window-enclosed front porch that, on a chilly day when the sun was out, became comfortably warm and lulling, especially if I had a book handy while my great-grandparents took a nap.

Kitty-corner to their house was the local firehouse — which is where, in hard times, Dorothy would haul my younger brother Drew and me on our rebuilt Radio Flyer wagon for the purpose of extracting surplus food in tan boxes. We were encouraged to do this because at that time my father was laid off from work, and we had only whatever money he could bring in doing odd jobs. The surplus food was stuff like dried eggs, powdered milk, blocks of orange cheese the size of Nazi gold ingots, corn meal, and canned meat — all of it probably left over from World War II. Dorothy used to mix up a pitcher of powdered milk and then pour in half a quart of real milk in an attempt to cut the chalky taste of the powdered milk. Unfortunately, the powder resisted being mixed with anything, and every once in a while we'd get a throat clogged with a powdered-milk clot.

It was this same firehouse where — during the shank-end of my grade-school career, when I worked after school on the Mauch Chunk Bakery delivery truck under the command of Shine Stermer — we'd end our late-afternoon bakery route. This last stop was not scheduled by mere accident or geography. Shine would invariably roll up in front of the bar entrance at the firehouse, pull a plastic-wrapped package of six hamburger buns from the shelf behind the driver's seat, and proclaim that he was going to check on the bar's supply of hamburger buns. (The bar served what was known as a barbecued sandwich: loose, cooked beef, grueled in a tomato-based sauce and slapped between a hamburger bun — sort of like a Manwich.)

It occurs to me all these years later that, in most states, volunteer fire companies don't each happen to have their own on-site bar the way they did, and still do, in Pennsylvania. In those days, nearly every able-bodied male (and some disabled) belonged to a fire company because, under Pennsylvania blue laws, public bars could not operate on Sundays, while firehouse bars and private "club" bars could.

"I'll be right back," Shine would announce around the Camel regular that constantly hung precariously from his lower lip, but never lost its ash.

"Okay," I'd say.

Once he was inside, I'd open my schoolbooks and begin to do some homework on the dash of the old Chevy panel truck. On occasion, Shine would be right back just as he'd said. But that was only on occasion — occasioned by what, I don't know, since it was the only stop on the route where I was *not* expected to personally make the delivery. Most days, though, Shine lingered inside, apparently counting and recounting hamburger buns to make certain that, should there be a flurry of barbecued sandwich activity, the bar would not come up short.

There were some particularly harsh winter evenings when the warmth of the great indoors and the accompanying warmth of the good fellowship inside caused the bun counting to go slowly — while outside, in the unheated cab of the bakery delivery truck, it was too dark to see my schoolwork and too cold to do much else but shiver and hope the weather didn't bring the wolves down out of the mountains. And there was no profit for me in the firehouse bun counting, because on weekdays after school I was on a set salary of fifty cents for what averaged out to two hours' work. There was no overtime pay, even if the firehouse stop went into a third or fourth hour and the lightly falling snow came up to the level of the truck's running boards.

My great-grandparents were dead by the time I began my career as Shine Stermer's lackey, so I couldn't go across the street to visit them and thaw out while Shine performed his hamburger-bun math inside the firehouse. The people who bought my great-grandparents' house filled in the goldfish pond with cement and let my great-grandmother's lush garden go to ruin. (As I recall from the *Ring* cycle, Valhalla — after the giants turned it over to Wotan — wasn't very well cared for either.)

The Dank Dark and Pistol Pete

My first look at what was to become the Benyo family mansion — 118 South Street, the uphill half of a double house — is smudged indelibly on my memory. Although I was only about fifteen months old at the time and knew nothing of Kafka or Dante, had the two ever met, our kitchen is where the meeting would have occurred.

Living under the roof of Peter and Mary Herman had become unbearable for everyone concerned. My memory isn't clear enough to recall whether my parents were motivated by their desire to escape the reins of the Herman reign, or whether the black sheep were *told* to leave because Dorothy had, for the second time, done the Big Dirty and was now pregnant with son number two — who would ultimately emerge as Andrew Joseph Benyo, Jr. (a.k.a. Drew). I suspect that both factions would have been able to tell the tale their own way and both would have been correct. As I was to learn, living inside The World According to Dorothy and Shorty, perception (and self-deception, even if delusional) was everything.

Since Dorothy was great of girth with Drew, it would probably have been the summer of 1947 when I got my first gander at the innards of 118 South Street. The house had been a rental; the owner apparently wanted to sell. The tenants — the Henritzys — didn't want to buy it, so they were thrown out, only to buy the next house up the street, 120 South Street. My parents took out a mortgage for something like four thousand dollars in order to become the proud owners of the way station to Hell. I was not consulted on the purchase. I spent most of my time during that period safely ensconced at the Herman household.

From photos that exist, it appears that I was having a fine old time at the Herman household up there on North Street, being the first-born boy and taking advantage of all the goodies that go with that accident of nature. I was apparently hogging it for all it was worth, and I vaguely remember being a supremely happy little white boy, even though the offspring of black sheep.

There are a number of photos of me from that period. In one, I'm sitting on my grandmother Mary's kitchen table at twelve months, grinning a goofy grin. (How I got onto the table, I have no idea. Seems unsanitary to me, especially considering the fact that I was probably not potty trained yet.) There's a photo of me, at seventeen-and-a-half months, sitting on the lawn with the family dog. (I was wearing dark brown shoes; I had a habit of dirtying and scuffing up every pair of shoes I ever wore.) In another, at seventeen-and-a-half months, I'm perched on Nana Herman's knee while she sits on the side/back porch. (I'm wearing the same dark brown shoes that hid the scuffs so well.) There's one at eight months of me in a snowsuit out behind the house standing in a rocker (shoes hidden); at one year, I'm sitting in the passenger seat of my Uncle Richie's car (no seatbelt, extremely scuffed white shoes, matching hat and coat); and, at eleven months, I'm being held by Pop-Pop (a.k.a. Gramps Peter Herman) in the backyard of their house, while wash dries on the line in the background (bare feet, no scuffs).

Come to think of it, if I was spending so much time being photographed at seventeen-and-a-half months at Peter and Mary Herman's house, we must have moved to 118 South Street in the fall of 1947, somewhat after Dot and Shorty fixed it up a bit, because Drew came along on December 2 that year. He was twenty months younger than I was. He still is.

In most of the homes with which we were familiar, the front room, or parlor, was inhabited by the most prized possessions and was kept uninhabited by human beings except on very special occasions, like post-funeral get-togethers and Christmas. And, since the parlor occupied the frontmost room on the first floor, this also ruled out the use of the perfectly functional front door. The front door, the door through which a normal person would consider entering a house, was kept locked. It was essentially as nonfunctional as the furniture in the parlor — except when there were very special guests on the premises. Look at it, but don't sit on it. (I understand that some cultures — among them the Italians — purchased plastic covers for the parlor furniture, so it would be museum quality five hundred years into the future.)

All commerce, commuting, entering, and exiting was done through the side door, which led to the kitchen. This madness was widespread. It infected people in Mauch Chunk, Summit Hill, Nesquehoning, Lansford, Coaldale, etc., and still does to some extent today — except for the new arrivals from metro areas (who know no better).

The only people from those days I recall who admitted human beings through the front door were people who were a little further up the social scale. I know this firsthand, because later in life, as I mentioned earlier, I worked as a kid delivering baked goods and as a result had occasion to visit at least one-third of all houses in East Mauch Chunk each and every Saturday. Some people actually *did* open their front doors to accept their Mauch Chunk Bakery delivery.

It is strong in my toddler memory that we entered the house from the side door. I remember a torrent of darkness, hanging things, darkness, ghosts, and more darkness.

Although this may be filling in memories with expectations of the event, I like to think the side door leading to the kitchen creaked open on rusted hinges. I believe it was late in the day, the side alleyway between 118 and 120 South Street, down which we walked, was in shadow. I suppose the Henritzys were looking out at us from behind curtains on the side of their new house watching us enter "their" house, for as I said before, it was my parents' prediction that we would forever be bedeviled by the Henritzys because we were moving into the house out of which we had caused them to be booted. In The World According to Dorothy and Shorty, a great deal of time and energy is expended imagining what other people will do or have done, and figuring out their motives — based entirely on projection—that is, based on what Dorothy and Shorty would think, feel, or do under the same circumstances. (In The World According to Dorothy and Shorty, everyone in the world was a shadow of Dorothy and Shorty.)

But, back to the cave. The door creaked open. A bit of breeze was brave or foolish enough to sneak inside, and things *moved!* I could see all of this because I was a lad of roughly fifteen months, and from my position way down low, I could see stuff adults missed. The place was eerie, black, and sinister, and there were things in there that were *moving!*

Shorty groped around on the wall to find the light switch. He turned it (it was one of those big old bulky round things that you turned, not something modern that you merely flicked on or off), and a dirty, bare 25-watt light bulb flickered on—a bare bulb suspended from the ceiling at the end of exposed wires, big bulky wires like desiccated garter snakes. The only heat in the house was provided by a big black coal stove over in the corner—near the doorway that opened to the stairs going down to the even darker cellar. Next to the stove, between its hulking self and the doorway to a darker hell, was the only running water in the house: a bare wash basin with exposed plumbing, the basin sort of attached to the wall.

A coal stove comes to life with the firing of anthracite coal and when anthracite coal burns, it produces a tremendous amount of soot. There was a rickety black tin chimney thing with the circumference of an Easter ham that went imperfectly up into the ceiling to get the smoke out of the house, but every time someone opened the stove to put in more coal or poke the embers, soot rose toward the ceiling. It may be an exaggerated estimate, but I think roughly one-fifth of the smoke and soot that the coal stove produced never left the kitchen. Consequently, everything within a half-mile of the stove was black, layer upon carbonized layer of soot, some of the deepest layers possibly already in the process of reconstituting to crude oil or prehistoric vegetation.

The soot had apparently reacted in some arcane way with the glue that held the wallpaper in place. What color and design the wallpaper had been on the day it had been hung was anybody's guess. By the time we first saw it, it was black. The ceiling had been wallpapered, and either the chemistry of the soot had undone the glue or else the very weight of the soot had become so extreme that it had pulled the paper from the ceiling despite the glue. The wallpaper on the ceiling hung loose in the middle, like so many horizontal black drapes. The breeze from the open door made the sooty black "wallpaper" billow and sway like the wings of giant black bats. I remember standing in the doorway, struck by a serious case of wonderment and terror. It was fantastic. We were going to live inside a cave with a moving ceiling!

I don't remember much about the tour of the rest of the cave. That first view of the kitchen was so overwhelming that it crushed out any other memories. Even today, I can overwhelm myself and put myself into a dark depression by recreating the scene of that door opening inward.

Of course a fifteen-month-old kid finds such horrors a sort of adventure, a fascination. I never thought to say either silently or out loud: "What a dump!" I had to be trained to make those judgments; I had to be coached by adults.

Today I can say it: "What a dump!"

The extent of the dumpiness became clearer as Shorty and Dorothy began working on the place. A painting and wallpaper guy, Shorty found—when he took the sprayer and putty knife to the kitchen wallpaper—that for eons, no one who had hung new wallpaper had ever bothered to scrape off the old stuff. They had merely pasted more wallpaper over the old layers until there were about a half-dozen layers to scrape through before getting down to the bare plaster. It was gruesome work. I helped out, applying a putty knife to a saturated little section of wall. I scraped and scraped as though I were scraping the scales off a particularly hardy dinosaur. The reptile analogy comes to mind because the water sprayed on the walls to soften the wallpaper made the room feel like it was inside an aquarium—an aquarium with the smell of damp plaster and wet coal soot.

Yes, today I can look back and say, "What a dump!" But that first day, I think all three of us said something else, even if not in so many words: "There's pride in home ownership."

The Black Sheep must have really, really, really been motivated to leave the home of Peter and Mary Herman. I wasn't in such a big hurry. I found myself connected to my grandparents' house sort of like the eons-old wallpaper was stuck to the kitchen walls at 118 South Street. I had three grandparents, and I was more interested in spending time with them than my black-sheep parents were.

My grandmother on my father's side was short. Her diminutive stature was compensated for by her overwhelming presence. She demanded attention by what I saw as her grouchiness. My father either outright inherited those traits or studied at her feet. Both could walk into a room filled with laughter and joy and squelch it without saying a word. My grandmother was, to us kids, scary. (My grandmother's passion in life was raising roses, but I've always been allergic to roses. Perhaps it's psychosomatic.)

Looking back at it though, I think it was more a discomfort with her old-country ways. Although she'd spent most of her life in the United States, she still clung to her East-European ways and frequently refused to speak English (although she was quite capable of doing so and had nine children who spoke English). In later life, my Aunt Anita, the youngest of the children, spoke fondly of my grandmother, remembering her warmth and charm. Different people, different perspectives. The baby of the family always has a unique take on Mom.

Grandma Benyo remarried, at one point, a nice enough fellow — a widower who had his own family. I recall that there was a lot of dissension among the Benyo family members about where the new guy stood, all of which was eventually ironed out to the satisfaction of *most* of the family. (Most.)

I've already mentioned that my grandparents on my mother's side were Peter and Mary Herman. Mary Herman ruled the roost. Tall, imposing, thin-lipped, Mary Herman always seemed impervious to life, very much bigger than life. Considering the dominance of my two grandmothers over their immediate environment, I would question the reputed patriarchy in America. I suspect both of those ladies would have sniffed at the concept. Since I was no sooner born than I was circumcised by a female doctor, perhaps I'm prejudiced. Or maybe I'm scared — at least of women wielding knives.

Then there was Peter "Pop-Pop" Herman. As a kid, I always used to think of Pop-Pop as *Pistol Pete*. He loved Western movies (and beer). Those were his passions, and on Saturdays he consumed them both with great vigor.

As a boy, Peter had been crippled when hit by a snowball in which another kid had hidden a rock. It hit Peter in the leg and the wound became so infected that he nearly lost that leg. For the rest of his life, Pete limped and lived in pain, always wrapped the leg in Ace-type bandages, and worked like a little locomotive. (I use the term *little* because Pete was shorter than his wife Mary. For their wedding picture, the photographer had Mary sitting and Peter standing so that the discrepancy in height would not be so obvious.)

Peter worked as janitor of St. Joseph's Parish, which included the church, the rectory, the grade school, and the nuns' residence — and the cemetery just outside of town. Winter and summer, he was up before the sun, stoking the fires so the little immigrant ladies in the parish wouldn't freeze in the huge church at the early (5:15 A.M.) Mass. When it snowed, Peter was up at church shoveling the pavements and sprinkling salt on the steps so people could get safely into church, then he shoveled the pavements around the school so the kids could get in to the good nuns to get their proper education.

The church was two uphill blocks away from Peter's house; he didn't have a car. He walked everywhere, but everything he needed was within a few blocks: the church, the grocery store, and the St. Joe's Club (the parish social club). Two of his sons who lived in town, Pudda (Poo-da) and Eppie (actually, Norbert and Edward, respectively), drove him anywhere he needed to go. The youngest son, Richie, taught high school math in Philadelphia, and usually came up on weekends. (This my parents resented, because Richie and his wife stayed at Peter and Mary's without paying — as though it were a motel. Did Peter and Mary charge Shorty, Dorothy, and me for staying under their roof for the first years of their marriage? They must have.)

By mentioning Peter's fondness for beer (a fondness genetically ingrained in most Germans — Nature once again over Nurture), it is certainly not to imply that he drank to excess. To a non-German it might have been drinking to excess. But, being German, Peter had learned his beer-drinking art from a young age, and he had learned it well. I never once saw Pop-Pop drunk, although on numerous occasions I saw him and his card-playing buddies drink beer from sunup to well past sundown. They also inherited bladders the size of swimming pools; they seldom left the card table once they started playing.

At parish picnics, Peter and his card-playing buddies would do ultra-marathon stints. It was the job of the grandsons to sprint between the card table and the beer stand in order to keep the elder gents supplied with cans of cold beer while they shuffled cards and shot the bull all day long.

They even had their own little social hideaway "out the country" (as we referred to anywhere above East Mauch Chunk in the direction of the Poconos). They had a clubhouse with a spring-fed pond. They kept kegs of beer chilled in the pond, and, on summer days, my cousin Dave and I had the job of diving into the freezing water to bring up the next keg to be tapped, while Pistol Pete and company played cards under the shade of an overhanging tree.

We drew pitchers of beer for the card-playing elders. They taught us to let the beer run down the side of the pitcher so it didn't generate too much of a head. They drank their beer from six-ounce glasses. Our job was to make sure the pitchers on the table were never empty, and we were each paid two dollars for our day's labor. There was nothing quite so satisfying to us kids as being the bartenders for the elder gents on a hot summer day, when all we needed to do to cool off was to fall into the pond.

Almost every time I have my first beer of the day, I think of my grandfather. He trained me, very patiently and proudly, to drink and appreciate beer.

In the days before Dorothy and Shorty broke down and bought a TV, which occurred when I was about eight years old, I used to spend Saturdays at Pistol Pete's, watching TV Westerns with him in the darkened front room. Saturday afternoons were about the only time in the whole week he didn't have to work, and those afternoon hours were his — or, rather, they were *ours*.

Although surrounded by mountains, we got excellent television reception. Our corner of Pennsylvania is where cable television originated. It started in Hazleton, where a bunch of appliance dealers, who couldn't sell televisions in their stores if nobody could get reception on them, banded together and built an antenna and then charged (rather exorbitantly) for people to get hooked up. (Running the cable around town must have been an expensive proposition.) Our area was the second in the world, after Hazleton, to get cable TV (called CATV in those days, meaning Community Antenna TV). The cable pulled in stations from New York City and Philadelphia, and one of the Philadelphia stations played cowboy movies all afternoon on Saturdays. The weekly cowboy marathon was sponsored by Earl Schieb — "We'll paint any car any color for $19.95!"

Peter would do his household chores on Saturday morning, and I'd help him cut grass and shovel coal into the coal bin by getting in his way. Of course, this was only after going through the weekly grilling from my grandmother about why my mother never visited. I don't know why; if they were both so damned curious about what the other was up to, why didn't they just visit each other and find out? Why put it on a seven-year-old kid? (Maybe the pressure from the older generations is why I took up drinking at such an early age.)

When noon on Saturday came, Pop-Pop would quit his working around the house, Mary would rustle up sandwiches for both of us, and we'd saunter into the front room and draw the shades. Then we'd watch Westerns all afternoon until suppertime. Pistol Pete would sit in the big stuffed chair, pour cold beer from the bottle into a glass, and sip his way through a Western double feature — sometimes, a triple feature. Our favorites were Tom Mix and Hopalong Cassidy. But he'd also accept Bob Steele, Roy Rogers, or Lash LaRue. He'd pour a six-ounce glass of beer for me, which I was expected to nurse for the afternoon. "Cuts the trail dust," he'd say. I'd always nod knowingly.

As a panoramic Western scene came on the little black-and-white TV screen and a stagecoach worked its way across from left to right, Pop-Pop would mutter, "Hain't that somethin'" — meaning the West. In his life, Peter Herman never got as far west as Pittsburgh, but the West was where his heart was.

At suppertime, as I'd leave to walk home, Pistol Pete insisted that I eat a piece of gum or a Sen-Sen to cover the smell of beer on my breath. "Don't tell your mother you've been drinking, or I'll never hear the end of it," he'd whisper. I never until now broke my word that I'd keep mum about Pistol Pete's influence on my enjoyment of the occasional barley pop. Thanks, Pop-Pop.

Drew

My younger brother, Andrew Joseph Benyo, Jr. was born on December 2, 1947. There were no hard-boiled eggs involved, but Extreme Unction (the Last Rites) was administered when his birth proved to be difficult. Being the feisty fellow he was, though, he made it through. I assume his feistiness was genetic (Nature) since he had not yet had much of an opportunity to be nurtured — and he wouldn't get much of that along the way, either.

Today, he's still feisty and is relatively healthy, other than a recurring back problem that resulted from an embankment collapsing on him while he was stationed in Alaska in the Air Force in the 1960s. In fact, in the summer of 1991, he ran/walked/stumbled from the peak of Mt. Whitney (14,494 feet above sea level) to Badwater in Death Valley (282 feet below sea level), a distance of one hundred fifty grueling miles. But I'm getting way, way ahead of the story.

After the nip-and-tuck drama of Drew's delivery, Dr. Jane Johnson told my parents that my mother's plumbing had been so compromised that she shouldn't even think of having any more children. Eight years later, she delivered Kathleen, and seventeen months after that, Barbara, before the plumbing gave out entirely. Dorothy had originally wanted to have twenty-six children, so she could name each one with a different letter of the alphabet. Jeez. Where would we all sleep? Which kid would be named Zebulon and which Xavier?

But back to Drew — number-two child, covering the letters A *and* D. (A twofer.)

In the snapshots that remain from that era, the photo that seems to me to have set the tone for the childhood relationship between

Drew and me is one taken a day or two after Drew was brought home from the hospital. I suppose that, to be cute about it, Dorothy and Shorty placed me on a doily-encrusted overstuffed chair and then placed a squealing, blanket-wrapped little monster on my lap. (Think of the film *Alien* where the fist-sized creature chews its way out of the guy's chest.) The infant's mouth is open in a scream very much like the ones Charles Schulz drew on his *Peanuts* characters when they were in the throes of great distress — the mouth opened wide enough to drive a train through. My expression is best summed up as stunned — or maybe shell-shocked. Put into words, my expression reads, "What the hell is this?"

In almost every way possible, Drew and I were opposites. He was outgoing, adventurous, daring, and impetuous, and liable to do spectacular (if often dumb-nut crazy) things, like jumping off the roof and running away from home when things didn't go well — which they seldom did. I was quiet (especially after my stuttering set in), reserved, cautious, and prone to thinking things through before jumping off a roof and running away from home. Hmmmm, should I take the red T-shirt or the blue one? Where's my toothbrush? How much peanut butter and crackers will I need?

Drew loved the Yankees; I followed the Phillies. He was a Rolling Stones fan; I was a Beatles fan. He collected his music in LP format; I bought 45s. He could whistle; I couldn't, so I hummed. He was picked first for ball games; I was picked last. He was popular in school; yeah.

When Dorothy became pregnant with Kathleen, Drew and I were moved to the unheated attic, which Shorty had converted into a bedroom. We got along so well that we got a roll of adhesive tape and divided the room in half. Neither of us was to cross into the other's territory — under pain of disembowelment. (Typical brothers.)

Yet for all the differences, we spent a fair amount of time together, shared the same South Street friends, messed around together, roamed Bear Mountain together, and later, cruised around with Catfish Gavornik in his old rattletrap '52 Plymouth. But we were always on different wavelengths, only occasionally in sync, and then not for very long. (Incidentally, our sisters, Kathleen and Barbara, had a similar relationship.)

I've always thought of Drew as the rebel, the madman. He'd pull off unexpected deeds, deeds he seemingly never thought through to their ultimate consequences — deeds, therefore, as unexpected and spectacular to him as they were to everyone else. I recall two of my favorites because they are so difficult to forget, even these many decades later.

Like many kids of that era, Drew and I were baseball card junkies. We spent endless hours trading cards we had for cards we desperately needed. The stakes for specific cards rose and fell based on the player's current performance, and ingenious trade deals brokered both on the table and under it. The value of certain cards was inflated, others devalued, on an almost hourly basis. Surveys were conducted and statistics examined to uncover patterns revealing which runs of cards tended to show up in which boxes in which store outlets throughout town. An incoming report of some much-needed card showing up at Joe Brown's Newsstand at Sixth and North streets would send a half-dozen glassy-eyed, panting kids careening around corners on their battered bicycles in hopes of hitting pay dirt.

As with any addiction, this one required a constant infusion of cash to meet the ever-escalating demands. During the summer months, we wore out our knuckles banging on doors of neighbors asking for odd jobs in exchange for the dirty lucre we needed to sate our fixations for Richie Ashburn and Mickey Mantle cards. Our parents saw it for the addiction that it was, and to the downfall of the nation's economy two decades later, did everything they could to force us to get rid of our addicting stash of cards. The economic future of literally hundreds of thousands of young men in America was destroyed by well-meaning parents who, during the kids' first year away at college or in the military, took the opportunity to haul the boxes of baseball cards to the local dump.

(It is ironic, isn't it, that our parents' generation, who so thoroughly made plans for their retirements, so lightly tossed ours aside. As soon as they could manage to do it, what were the three things they tossed out? Baseball cards. Comic books. Rock'n'roll records. Not too long ago, a copy of the first issue of *Batman* comics sold for nearly a hundred thousand dollars. And, to make the idiocy complete, which of our motley possessions did our parents save for us? Our high school report cards — which might be worth a few bucks to the *National Enquirer* only if we become president of the United States or a serial killer.)

In order to keep my baseball card collection growing and my right cheek filled with sweet, pink, tooth-rotting baseball-card gum, I made arrangements with grandmother Mary Herman to spend Saturday mornings doing chores: running to the grocery store, mowing the lawn, shoveling coal into the coal hopper, extracting ash cans from the tidy basement — whatever it took to end up with silver coins in my sweaty palm at day's end. Extremely mercenary stuff. By 2:00 on a Saturday afternoon, I was on my bike sniffing for the latest statistical rumors relative to which local outlet's supply of baseball cards was turning up an unnatural run of Philadelphia Phillies cards.

One particular Saturday afternoon, as I was finishing up my chores at Mary Herman's house, a-sheen with kid-sweat that comes with honest but frantic work — especially frantic today because it was the day the third series of Topps baseball cards for that summer was to reach the stores — Mary Herman came up from behind and startled me. "You've been working really hard today," she said. "Here's an extra" — and she plopped into my open palm a bonus, hefty half-dollar — "something for you." But she wasn't finished. She dropped in another half-dollar that clanged against the first with an almost sexual satisfaction. "This one's for your brother."

The first thing that nearly came spewing out of my mouth was, "But... he didn't do any work!" However, I held my vile tongue in check — which was relatively easy for a stutterer, a creature who seldom speaks prematurely. I reconsidered such a selfish sentiment and kept quiet, buttressed by the thought that such largesse on Mary Herman's part might actually induce Drew to consider coming along with me the next Saturday to help get the chores finished that much faster. (Drew seldom went to Mary Herman's, possibly an indication that he had more black-sheep genes that I did.)

"Wow! Thanks!" I gushed, a picture in my head of the smooth waxed-paper covers of the nickel packs of baseball cards that were waiting for me; the sweet powdery residue from the gum sticking to the inside of the packs, pure ambrosia; the ritual of undressing each pack individually until it revealed its innermost secrets — the anticipation perversely drawn out in a ritual that would four years later be reserved for fantasies of undressing tassel-sneakered cheerleaders a year or two my senior. I ran my bicycle down the backyard, did a flying mount — just as I imagined Pony Express riders had done a century before — and powered myself home in a terror of excitement.

As fate would have it, I encountered Drew coming in the other direction, lumbering up Center Street as though he had the weight of the world on his shoulders, in one of his darkly moody moods, who-knows-*what* going through the vexed corridors of his mind. I slammed on the brakes, skidded to a dramatic stop, held out his manna, and told him from whence it had fallen. He looked at the shiny fifty-cent piece, took it, and walked on, as though he'd been expecting something just like this to happen — sort of like if the Publishers Clearing House prize patrol knocked at your door and you ushered them in to brunch, saying, "Please do come in. We've been expecting you. I do hope you like bagels and cream cheese."

For some reason, I don't recall why, I was detained at home, not allowed to go to the store to make my simply huge purchase of nickel packs of baseball cards. I was probably being punished for some imagined transgression. I hadn't even been home all day so I *could* get into trouble. (If there was one thing we could always count on at our house, it was to not count on anything.)

The next day, the subject of the fifty-cent-piece bonuses came up. Mary Herman had mentioned it to my mother when they'd briefly spoken on the phone. "What did you do with the money?" Dorothy asked. Since I'd been restrained at home the previous day, I dove into my jeans pocket and pulled out my half-dollar — along with half a piece of Wrigley's Spearmint gum, some lint, and a few pennies.

"Where's yours?" Dorothy asked Drew.

"I didn't get no half-dollar," he said, his face as straight as a parish priest's just leaving a High Mass.

"You da-da-did too," I said, certain he was trying to be funny. "I ga-ga-gave it to you yesterday when I sa-sa-sa-saw you a-a-a-on Center Street."

"No you didn't," he insisted.

"Da-da-da-did too!" I said, feeling the complexion of the day taking on a sticky pallor.

"Did not!" he shot back.

I was expected to shoot back with another "Did too!" but something in the changing atmosphere held me back. I didn't want to escalate the situation. We'd just been to church an hour before, and I was still at the age when I was cautious that if I did anything untoward too close to having been to church, the punishment was multiplied — by like twelve or so. It was better to wait until church wore off a bit.

"We'll get to the bottom of this *when your father gets home*," Dorothy said.

My father always went to visit his two hunting buddies after church on Sunday mornings, then came home and complained for hours about them. My mother had the perpetual habit of not punishing us when an offense was fresh. Instead, she took note of it, and promised that our punishment would come when Shorty got home, which sometimes wasn't going to be for another eternity or two, which meant that we had six or seven hours to suffer in anticipation of the actual physical beating.

By the time he did get home, of course, the punishment would not be based on the actual offense, which was usually incredibly minor, but would instead be based on what kind of a day Shorty had had at work — at the No. 8 machine shop of the Bethlehem Steel Company. I don't recall him coming home from work in a good mood very often. Shorty was one of those guys who knew how to do everything better than everyone else — including the president of Bethlehem Steel — even though his own little painting and paperhanging company had gone bankrupt. (But there was absolutely no doubt what kind of mood he'd be in when he came home from Dreck and Joey's houses. It was a ritual, as predictable as the sun's rising and setting.)

Mid-afternoon finally arrived, after about three hundred years; Shorty was home. As per usual, things had not gone well at Joey Angolovich's house. Joey and Dreck Bimler were what passed as Shorty's friends. The three of them occasionally went hunting together, and they all got together at Joey's or Dreck's after mid-morning Sunday Mass for coffee and camaraderie — or whatever passed for camaraderie. (If Mass at St. Joseph's Catholic Church was meant to soothe the souls of the just and the unjust, the post-Mass get-together at Joey's was the devil's work.) Shorty was not the type to tell someone what he thought of him (or of what that person was saying) to his face. He'd fume and simmer and then come home and treat us to what he would have said — what he *should* have said, but didn't.

Drew and I were huddled in our attic bedroom maturely discussing the day's events:

"I da-da-da-did sa-so ga-ga-give you the ma-ma-money!"

"You did *not!*"

"Did *so!*"

"Did *not!*"

When we heard the crunch of gravel under the tires of our father's car out front, all dialogue ceased. A blood-pressure gauge strapped to either of us would have blown its top at that point. For both the experienced and the overly sensitive, it was possible to discern Shorty's state of rage by how hard he applied the brakes when he pulled up out front. We listened intently. I turned to Drew. "Na-na-now ya-ya-you're in ta-ta-ta-trouble," I breathed.

We could hear nearly every word as they spiraled up the stairways from two floors below, like ghosts escaping Earth's gravity. Dorothy's sketching of the offense took a bit longer than usual because it was a hair more complex than the usual. This wasn't "He slammed the screen door" and should therefore undergo at least an hour of the red-hot thumbscrews.

"You two get your asses down here *now!*" came up the attic stairs like a blast of brimstone from an erupting inferno. There was a mad rush to see who could be last going down the stairs. There was definitely, absolutely, positively no doubt whatsoever as to what Shorty's mood was. The wallpaper in the stairwell began to smolder, paint on the stairway began to blister, the gates of Hell swung open on all-too-smooth hinges, and the smell of brimstone was in the air.

I continue to be astonished that Andrew "Shorty" Joseph Benyo, Sr. lived as long as he has — how he got through so many years without just outright blowing a gasket or two. His face was red, he was in his patented action-crouch, the veins on his head bulged out like sewer lines, and smoke issued from his ears like it did from the stacks of a Mississippi riverboat under a full head of steam.

He lined us up side by side, like he always did under these circumstances — a habit left over from his years as an officer in the United States Army — as if he were lining up traitors against a wall to shoot them. The tears were already welling up behind my eyes, about to, once again, aggravate an already tense situation. I didn't want to see Drew get beaten to within an inch of his life as I'd seen a few other times, and I knew my tears, when they came, would only stimulate Shorty more. They worked like dropping battery acid on an outstretched tongue. (Dorothy stood in the doorway, effectively heading off Drew's usual bolt for the exit.)

Shorty questioned us on the particulars of the crime. Of course, our separate renditions of the particulars didn't jive in the least little bit. I insisted that I had given Drew the fifty-cent piece Mary Herman had given *to* me *for* him. But Drew insisted I hadn't.

"It doesn't take a genius to see that one of you is a goddamned liar," Shorty deduced, his mind extra sharp — due no doubt to being intellectually stimulated by talking with Joey and Dreck. (Dorothy had winced at his use of *goddamned* — it being Sunday and all.) "And before the day's over," he continued, "I'll get to the bottom of this." He straightened up in a dramatic fashion, a judge about to announce a decision. "Go out to the kitchen and move the table against the wall." This sounded more dangerous than the usual beating-to-within-an-inch-of-your-life. I glanced around furtively to see if he'd pulled out any of his hunting rifles to finish us off.

We shuffled out to the kitchen like two condemned prisoners shackled together and bound for the scaffold. We did as we were told, then stood stupidly in the middle of the kitchen floor.

(The kitchen had been greatly improved since the first day the four of us — Drew, still in utero — walked into it. There was now a proper kitchen sink, kitchen counters, kitchen cupboards, an actual gas range, and even a refrigerator — of some years' age, but still in serviceable condition. The kitchen had been repapered and the bare wood floor covered with linoleum.)

Drew and I gazed suspiciously at each other from under bowed heads. What the hell was going on here? My gaze was becoming a little fuzzy from the tears that slid out and splattered on the (always waxed) linoleum floor. "Kneel down," Shorty said. We did. I had read a lot of Crusades books and knew how captured Crusaders had their heads lopped off by an Arab with a scimitar. I felt a knot in my throat. "You're going to kneel here until one of you admits he lied, even if it takes all day."

Where he learned this punishment I'm not certain, but it must have been in the military. I'd seen POWs in Japanese camps who were made to kneel all day long in the hot sun. I'd also seen a picture of a POW kneeling, his hands tied behind his back, just before his head was to be separated from his shoulders by a sword as tall as the executioner. Scimitar or samurai sword, what's the difference? The result is the same.

We knelt side by side on the cold kitchen floor while my parents proceeded through the day as though this were exactly what happened around here every Sunday afternoon — and there were not two kids kneeling in the middle of the kitchen floor. Newspapers were shuffled, knitting needles clicked and clacked, and an occasional conversation drifted dimly in from the living room. The afternoon wore on. Every so often, Drew and I screwed up enough courage to confront each other at a sideways angle. "Tell the truth," I implored, "or I'll get you for this!" — as though a crying kid was much of a threat to anything or anybody.

"I'll get *you* for this," Drew threatened back.

I was none too pleased with this particular punishment. In the whole scenario, the flaw that Shorty had overlooked was that he was dealing with two professional kneelers, two veteran altar boys from St. Joseph's Church — altar boys who had, on numerous occasions, made it through a Requiem High Mass. (There, when the congregation kneels the altar boys kneel, when the congregation stands, the altar boys stand, and when the congregation sits, the altar boys *kneel*, for hours, in uncomfortable costumes). I had, on several occasions, felt myself passing out while kneeling in the heat of an August High Mass while trapped, broiling, inside a wool cassock. What was most punishing wasn't the kneeling. It was watching the shadows outside the kitchen windows indicate dramatically that a perfectly good Sunday afternoon was lumbering on by while we were polishing the linoleum with the knees of our blue jeans.

Supper came and Dorothy turned on the lights. She moved around the kitchen and made supper, walking around us as though we were part of the furniture. Shorty and Dorothy sat down to eat at the kitchen table which was still pushed against the wall. That night, as always, Shorty ate his supper as though, if he didn't eat with the speed of a seagull, someone was going to steal the food right from under his chin. (He claimed it was due to growing up in a large family where, if you didn't fight for your portion and gulp it down fast, you'd go hungry.) After supper, Dorothy cleaned up while Shorty went into the next room and read ads for Winchester .30-30 rifles in his *American Rifleman* magazine — his primary reading material. The shadows grew long and sinister, the day waned, and night came on with a rush. And we still knelt, intermittently egging each other on to own up and tell the truth (or else).

Shorty's interrogation plan was not going well at all, and that kind of thing only served to anger him more. I guess enough time had gone by that a few brain cells lined up and he cooked up a new angle to the torture. He opened the cellar door and reached behind it for the coal shovel, which hung there on a nail. My immediate fear was that he was going to begin to whack us upside the head with it. But, no, he went down the cellar steps, scraped around down there for a while, then clambered back up with the shovel heaped with ashes from the furnace. Since he'd scooped them up from the top of the ash barrel that was still inside the furnace (I'd emptied the barrels down at The Dump after church), the ashes were still hot. He poured the ashes carefully across the linoleum floor in front of us and ordered us to move forward and kneel on the ashes.

Three weeks prior to this, in St. Joseph's School, we'd studied the sanitized version of the Spanish Inquisition. It was a Catholic school, after all, dedicated to sparing us the horrors one set of human beings had perpetrated on another in the name of Holy Mother Church. My kneecaps, as they attempted in vain to adapt themselves to the sharp edges of unburned coal mixed in with warm ash, quickly became students of the Shorty Inquisition. Drew and I attempted, each in his own way, to settle in for another long haul. I shifted my weight back and forth, giving one knee a break, then the other; I leaned back in an attempt to rest my butt on the heels of my shoes to take some of the strain off my knees and my lower back.

In desperation, I actually considered saying that I'd kept the fifty cents. This whole scene had become absurd. We already knew we weren't going to get any supper and were going to be sent to our rooms early; we'd already missed *The Ed Sullivan Show*. For consolation, I had a perfectly good Philip K. Dick novel waiting for me up in my room and, ya know, altar-boy training aside, my knees were beginning to give out.

But I just couldn't bring myself to put an end to the whole idiotic exhibition. That genetic joining of German pigheadedness and Slovak stubbornness had spawned something truly epic in Shorty's sons. So I decided to work to break Drew down. And I got down and dirty about it immediately.

"Look, you lousy son-of-a-bitch, tell the truth and get this shit over with or I'll make you wish you'd never been born." (Even at that age, Drew was bigger and stronger than I was, but I could still beat the shit out of him because I fought smarter. However, I had absolutely no idea of how I'd make him wish he'd never been born. I'd have to think on that one for a while.)

"You liar!" he cried. "You never gave me the money!" I could tell by the whine creeping into his voice that he was weakening, his resolve unraveling. I'd been an altar boy longer than he had and having seniority, I'd served at more Requiem High Masses than he had. Experience was beginning to tell.

By this time my knees were pretty numb. There were no more sharp pains. I felt my lower legs going to sleep, and thought that if I didn't get off them soon, they'd have gone too long without blood — gangrene would set in, and they'd probably have to be amputated. All over fifty goddamned cents!

The sound of our dialogue reached Shorty's eager ears as muffled mumbling.

"Are you two ready to tell me the truth?" he shouted.

"Na-na-no," I said stupidly.

"You're gonna stay there as long as it takes," he reminded us.

I began to work on Drew to break him down with words rather than threats. (I don't remember exactly what I said, but when I saw the scene in *Silence of the Lambs* where Hannibal Lecter talks Muggs into taking his own life, my familiarity with that heartlessness sent a shiver of recognition through me.) Within forty minutes, Drew began to whimper — and then to cry. Shorty came to investigate the change in atmosphere emanating from the darkened kitchen, and, through a gallon of snot, Drew blew out his confession. "I lied," he cried. "I spent the money."

I felt drained, almost dead inside, as though the wind had been knocked out of me by a quick punch to my solar plexus. There was no feeling of victory, of justice served, of triumph — just an empty hollowness that echoed eerily, and confusion about why it had to come to this.

Shorty dragged Drew by the elbow and began whipping him through the kitchen, through the living room, and up the stairs. Drew went up, screaming at the top of his lungs. I was left to sweep the ashes off the kitchen floor. "Sweep up the floor!" Shorty had growled through clenched teeth. I swept up the finely crushed ashes with a whiskbroom, took them out into the alleyway, and poured them into the sticky hedges. I limped back inside and stood in the middle of the kitchen; the bright lights that were now on seemed to accuse me of something, as though I were in a police lineup.

Dorothy came out and turned off a few of the lights. I began to limp away, wanting nothing more than to get out of that kitchen dungeon of terror, to get upstairs to bed. I had the coal shovel in my hand, ready to rehang it behind the cellar door, when Shorty returned and proceeded to tell me that he and Dorothy had known all along that I had given Drew the fifty cents, but that he'd had to punish me too in order to get Drew to admit what he'd done.

I understood not one dust mote of that logic. Whatever the hell his rationale was for all that had happened, it was totally foreign to the way I saw the world.

"You can go up and hit your brother for what he made you go through," Shorty said, as though that were my consolation prize. I was stunned — stunned that my father and I were so remote from each other on what was fair and just, and what was not. What I wanted to do at that moment was apply the coal shovel to the side of my father's head in an attempt to knock some sense into it. I looked up at him with a look I'm sure he didn't understand, took the coal shovel to the cellar stairway, hung it on its nail, closed the cellar door as gentle as a breeze, and marched upstairs to the bedroom Drew and I shared. (And I wondered about how deep I'd have to dig to unearth the old outhouse pit so I could bury Shorty's body.)

Drew was whimpering under his covers and making vague threats, at which I merely snorted. I turned on my bedside light and read in the Philip K. Dick novel of a world that was almost as weird as the one I currently inhabited, while Drew continued to curse and bluster into his pillow. Of course, by the next day, Drew and I were back to our usual, weirdly average, brotherly relationship.

The other incident that comes to mind is a real beaut. It is the misadventure where Drew and his buddy, Georgie "Puppy" Armbruster, became the kings of the ironclad alibi. (Riiiiiiight.)

One summer, as soon as school was out, the band of boys from South Street extracted permission from Catfish Gavornik's parents to build a tree house on the big tree at the end of their backyard just above the edge of The Dump. At this point, Catfish and his family lived in a ramshackle old two-and-a-half-story, tarpaper-sided house a block up South Street from us. (The house hasn't been there for decades. It eventually wore out and was torn down, and a new house was built there. This story concerns how it almost vanished before its time.)

The band of boys (known as The South Street Gang — more like the Little Rascals–type gang than the Bloods or the Crips) gathered together every spare piece of lumber we could beg, borrow, or steal from the local lumberyard. We used some really big pieces of wood as the base of the tree house, and the hammering and rope-tying and support-bracing and general construction melee went on at a furious pace for days. There's no more raw energy source than a band of pre-teens with a project of their own invention, especially if it makes them feel older than they are — which, having your own house swaying in the trees will do.

Within three days, with an old, huge, canvas tarp pulled over the whole thing as a roof, the project was finished. The tarp was army olive green and blended nicely with the tree's leaves. From a mile or two away, on a cloudy day, you'd never know the tree house was there. We had a ladder that operated on hinges so we could let it down with ropes (like a drawbridge) that touched upon the edge of the bank. And even though we weren't using our palace after dark, we had a supply of candles (just in case). We were in that stage of boyhood where fire was one of our prime gods.

Unfortunately, there was a fatal flaw with our engineering. All of that additional weight — two-by-fours, four-by-fours, eight-by-tens, books, candles, tarps, plus our own bodies, including Catfish's considerable bulk — was too much for the old tree. At the point where the two primary branches formed the Y in which we'd braced the tree house, we detected a crack — a crack that was growing by the hour.

We rushed in a frenzy to the service station on Fourth Street that Catfish's dad ran, in order to get his permission to relocate the tree house to the big tree that grew beside the Gavornik castle. Saddled with two gas customers, a brake job on a '53 Buick that had seen better days, three snot-nosed kids wanting to buy nickel Cokes, three tire-repair jobs, and a ball-bearing salesman who wouldn't leave, Gavornik *pere* quickly gave his permission and was immediately rid of at least one distraction.

It took us another three days to tear down the original tree house, bang straight all the nails we'd hammered through our supply of stolen lumber, move everything over to the new tree, hoist it up *into* the new tree, and reassemble it. Because the two trees were configured very differently, there were some serious engineering adjustments required, which involved customizing some of the lumber we'd originally cut and trimmed. But finally it was finished, a monument to kid ingenuity. (I refer architects and design experts in the audience to any of several Our Gang clubhouses to get an approximation of our genius.)

We began holding meetings whenever we could get everyone together. I had part-time work three days a week and all day Saturday on the bakery truck. Catfish was required to help out at his father's service station (primarily pumping gas and doing janitorial stuff). There were lawns to be cut, gardens to be dug, baseball games to be played. But the tree house became the central gathering place. There were almost always kids there, hanging out, reading comic books, lazing around, and feeling like big shots with their own cool-guy pad. Life was good.

One afternoon, one of the neighbors noticed smoke coming out of the tree house; then there were flames; then there was a fire truck. There was immediate concern that the flaming tree house was going to catch the Gavornik house on fire; there was some singeing of the tarpaper siding; then it was all doused by the firemen. Finally, there was the aftermath.

How'd the fire get started? The remnants of candles were found in the damp debris. Who'd been there to start the fire? The usual suspects were rounded up.

It was a Saturday, so I had spent the day running baked goods into peoples' houses. Catfish had spent the day at his father's garage getting caught up on repairing a mountain of bald-eagle used tires for resale. Georgie Armbruster claimed to have been uptown playing basketball, but he was a little vague on the details and the names of the guys with whom he'd been playing.

Catfish was livid about the fact that "his" tree house had been burned down. Mr. Gavornik was livid about the fact that his *real* house had nearly burned down. And I was livid about the stash of perfectly good comic books that had been first, burned, and then, drowned.

Drew, when questioned, had an alibi: He'd been — Stop the presses! — at the library! All afternoon, on a perfectly gorgeous Saturday, my one and only brother, whose interest in school hinged mainly on sports and girls, *had been at the library.*

The neighbor who had seen the smoke said that, before she saw the smoke, she'd seen two boys running away from the tree house, but she couldn't tell which two boys it had been; they all looked pretty much alike to her. (Obviously, she was a proto-racial profiler. We were all very much unalike.)

My brother continued to contend that he'd been *at the library.* The library to which he was referring was on the other side of town, on Broadway. (You remember — geography.) To get there, you had to walk two blocks downhill, cross the bridge over the Lehigh River, walk another quarter-mile along the railroad tracks to Broadway, and then up Broadway two blocks. Although walking that far was not unusual for most of us, for Drew to walk that far just to open a book on a beautiful Saturday afternoon stretched the ol' credibility like Silly Putty.

The questioning continued, the consequences spelled out by the respective fathers escalated like the pot in a poker game, and before the stakes got too high, Georgie Armbruster broke. Yes, he and Drew had been in the tree house. Yes, they'd been using the candles. Yes, they set one of the candles too close to the old surplus canvas tarp. Yes, it had caught fire — really, really fast; you shoulda seen it! Yes, they'd panicked and run — in opposite directions. Yes, yes, yes. We'll sign the confession. Anything!

My aging memory doesn't readily regurgitate the punishments that were meted out by enraged fathers. But ultimately, the entire gang was punished, because it was declared by the assembly of fathers that there would be no more tree houses that summer — or ever. And, certainly, *no more candles.*

For a week or two, Drew and George were pariahs. They were forced to walk our mean streets alone, friendless. But kids have short memories. (It is only as we age, it seems, that our memories expand to retain all affronts.) By the end of the summer, everything had blown over and all was back to whatever passed for normal in those days.

As I look back over my description of these episodes, it occurs to me that I may have painted my brother Drew in a color I didn't intend. It sounds as though he was a terrible fellow, always getting into trouble. Actually, he was — and still is — a damned good brother. It's just that his transgressions, like Huck Finn's, stand out above his positive accomplishments, maybe because those transgressions were so spectacular.

I want it to be perfectly clear that I hold my brother in high regard. It isn't that he was ever consciously bad. It is more that Drew was the kind of kid who acted first — without aligning all available brain cells to assess the potential outcomes of his actions. People used to joke that he'd been dropped on his head when he was little. (Dorothy sometimes offered the possibility that during his difficult birth he may have missed out on a bit of oxygen.) And the Henritzys used to refer to Drew as *Doozy*, an homage to his left-of-center exploits. (Did I mention that he's left-handed?)

Plotting

As a four-year-old kid, I was drowned in Little Golden Books, and what a way to go! I had one of the most extensive libraries of Little Golden Books in the world — everything from *The Little Engine That Could* to *Little Black Sambo*.

Those Little Golden Books, or most of them anyway, were given to me by Phyllis Henritzy — not to be confused with Lewie and Ellie Henritzy who lived one door up from us. Phyllis Henritzy lived down the street, on the same side, at what would have been 108 South Street. She lived with a lot of other Henritzys (Helen, Lois, May, etc.) in what Drew and I would later refer to as The House of Women. The house hosted a mélange of aunts and nieces and great-aunts and first and second cousins once or twice removed, about a half-dozen in all — all women of various ages and stages, all widowed or never married, two or more in wheelchairs, all wonderful women who kept a gimbaled eye on the South Street neighborhood to make sure it ran smoothly. They were like a gaggle of female sheriffs.

Phyllis Henritzy, of whom I write, worked across town on Broadway, in the Five-and-Ten-Cent store — or, as we used to call it, The Five 'n' Dime. Since Dorothy and Shorty were struggling financially (Shorty was periodically unemployed after his own painting and wallpaper company went belly-up, and then was unemployed on a seasonal basis when Drew Culley's painting and paperhanging company's work was slow), the Henritzy ladies took an interest in our welfare. Their concern extended to feeding the mind as well as feeding the belly.

Through a series of convenient coincidences, Phyllis Henritzy, bless her, fed my addiction for books. She was paid at The Five 'n'

Dime on Fridays, and every Friday she bought me a new Little Golden Book with her employee's discount. She walked to and from work, a distance of about a mile each way, crossing the bridge over the Lehigh River — at that time the old scary bridge with the splintered and broken wooden planks on the walkway. On her way home from work on Friday afternoon, she'd walk right on past her own house and come uphill to 118 South Street, knock on the door (the side door, of course), and come in to visit with Dorothy for a few minutes. This regular Friday afternoon visit had been going on for about a year and had become a ritual. But, since my parents were so antisocial, I was nearly always surprised to see any visitor in our house.

After that short visit with Dorothy, Phyllis Henritzy would get down on the floor and play with me for a few minutes, then she'd pull her purse over to us and she'd make a great game out of rummaging around in it until she found, as if to her own great surprise — and definitely to my delight — the next installment of my growing library. She handed the book to me as though it really were made of gold. I acted surprised every time, because I genuinely was, since I had absolutely no idea what book would appear next.

My far-and-away favorite was *The Little Engine That Could*, a rip-roarin' adventure with a plotline worthy of a 420-page Russian novel. There have been precious few novels written in the history of the world that have come even close to its brilliance. Today, in our politically correct world, I'm sure the novel is shunned because the little locomotive succeeded in accomplishing something important through sheer perseverance — which would have made all the engines that didn't care enough to give it the old college try a case of deflated self-es-steam. The book, therefore, should be banned.

As I received the new book and held it in my pudgy little hands, I'd say thank you as I'd been taught, I'd study the cover, run my fingers over the bright colors, and attempt to intuit the subject from the cover painting. Then I'd open it carefully and scan a few of the opening pages. I'd mumble a few words to myself that I recognized. Then I'd invariably utter the request that made us all happy: "Read some . . ."

When I flashed my winning smile there wasn't much else Phyllis could do. She straightened her skirt, settled in on the floor with me in that fluid way women can lower themselves and men can't, I snuggled up against her hip, and she turned the pages with an exaggerated slowness, while enunciating every word in a way that, at four, I found very sexy.

When Phyllis finished the book and left, Dorothy returned to making supper and I plotted how I was going to waylay her after supper to get her to read the book again. (Dorothy patiently read to Drew and me so often — reading and rereading the same books — that we both learned how to read by the age of five, merely by memorizing the Little Golden Books and then reading them to ourselves out loud and matching the words we said with the words on the page.)

The Little Golden Book library was housed in the back upstairs room, where Dorothy did her ironing and sewing. It was not unusual for me to amuse myself for hours at a time paging through the books and pretending that I was reading them to myself. Predictably, this practice had a dangerous side effect. It promoted a vivid imagination.

One afternoon Dorothy was working downstairs and I suppose Drew was taking a nap or was outside playing. I had the Little Golden Books spread over the floor. I also had sheets of scrap paper on one side, on whose clean side I practiced my skills as a young artist. I used my box of Crayola crayons to color in my drawings. But I never colored in a Little Golden Book. That was just not done.

This particular afternoon, my imagination got the best of me. I began, in my mind, to mix and match the characters from the Little Golden Books. I'd read the books so many times the way they were written that I sort of began to rewrite them. I imagined that Donald Duck boarded the Little Engine That Could and headed for the mountains; along the way the engine stopped at a station and picked up Popeye; and halfway up the mountain, they saw Little Black Sambo running from the tigers and tried to save him. I went so far as to mumble new dialogue to myself. "Run as fast as you can, Sambo!" Popeye called out of the side of his mouth as he jumped from the train, looking around frantically for some spinach. Meanwhile, Donald Duck, in his usual fashion, jumped up and down, a frantic wreck. I moved the books this way and that way, trying to get them lined up the way the new plotline was taking shape in my mind, but it just wasn't working. Then I spotted the little plastic, kid-scissors lying on top of my latest Crayola masterpiece. Well, I thought to myself, here's the answer.

Dorothy must have hoped I'd fallen asleep while reading. It was incredibly quiet upstairs, and I suppose she thought to herself: Ah! Some peace for a change. Why interrupt a good thing? I believe it took me roughly ninety minutes to carefully cut out the various characters from a dozen of the books. Using plastic scissors to cut around a character's hair is really tough. Fortunately, when you're dealing with Donald Duck and Popeye, there isn't much hair to slow you down. I laid the characters out on the floor — moving them this way and that — into the variations my mind required to fulfill a certain plot twist.

When they were arrayed around the floor as carefully as Shakespeare had plotted *Titus Andronicus*, Dorothy came up the stairs. She is gonna love this, I thought. I've made a bigger, better Little Golden Book — A Great Big Little Golden Book!

As she came around the corner, I looked up — beaming — secure in the knowledge that what I'd done was nothing short of brilliant. Dorothy's jaw fell roughly three feet. She was obviously impressed. But it seemed like seven or eight minutes passed while her dislocated jaw just sort of hung there. (This reaction wasn't exactly pumping up my pride in authorship.) When she found the next intake of breath for which she'd been desperately searching, she went crazy. Big-time crazy.

She grabbed my wrist and lifted me straight up. I was levitating. She tore the plastic scissors from my hand. And with one roar of disapproval she became my toughest literary critic ever. My punishment was swift. I was confined to my room for the rest of the day and into the night, with all my toys removed. This left me alone with the most dangerous toy of all: my own brain.

Of course (ask anyone who collects stuff — any stuff), once a bad habit is begun, it's damned difficult to break. I continued to mix disparate characters, and the habit stuck with me. As I moved to books without pictures — especially the Grosset & Dunlap boys' adventure books — Frank and Joe Hardy joined Tom Corbett, Tom Swift, Jr., and Rick Brant on adventures their authors never imagined. Consequently, I was already primed when, in the early '60s, the DC Comics superheroes came together to fight evil as The Justice League of America.

Heck. What if we took the concept global? Wouldn't it be great if someday all the countries of the world could get together and — all for one and one for all — work together? Geography would finally be rendered irrelevant. (I sure can dream them up, can't I?)

Ether Or

Each generation of kids goes through its own unique barrage of diseases. Today, it seems there is an epidemic of diseases we never saw when we were kids — stuff like asthma — some of which may be due to raising kids in what amounts to a sterile environment. The kids today never get a chance to develop antibodies.

You don't see many kids making and eating mud pies these days, for instance. Mud pies are probably an antidote to asthma. I don't recall knowing any kid who suffered from asthma. Polio, sure; we all knew of a kid or two who was diagnosed with polio. But they eventually gave us vaccines or magic sugar cubes for that.

They developed vaccines for a lot of other things, too, from TB and measles to chicken pox and mumps. Of course, some of the marvelous shots came *after* the fact — after we'd suffered days of slick-sweat fever in a darkened room with scabs forming over the lesions from the chicken pox. "But I never touched a chicken. Honest!"

One childhood "disease" you don't hear much about these days is tonsillitis. In the early '50s, any sign of inflammation in the throat called for the immediate removal of a kid's tonsils, remember? And often it was even done prophylactically.

At the age of five, I developed an inflammation in my throat, so Dorothy and Shorty took me to see the family doctor, Doc Dougherty (the M.D., not his brother the D.D.S.). Together, they decided I'd better be admitted to the Palmerton Hospital — once again under the direction of Doctor Jane, the same one who delivered and circumcised me — to have my tonsils removed. And, since *I* was going in, they decided to send Drew along to get his tonsils out at the same time so they wouldn't have to go through this whole thing again the following year when *his* throat would, no doubt, become inflamed. It was the buddy system, a two-fer-one, but neither of us was eager to go to the hospital, a dozen miles away, that we had escaped at birth (Drew, just barely).

Our parents sat us down and gave us — a five- and a four-year-old — a sort of combination pep talk and ultimatum. What we're doing is good for you and you'll like it and cooperate, or else.

But Drew and I were firm in our little resolves not to go along with this. One reason was that, as black sheep, our parents didn't much socialize, and therefore — other than playing with the neighborhood kids — we were not very accustomed to the larger world. They'd be abandoning us in a strange town many miles from home, and our mother — no doubt reflecting her own fears of the big wide horrible world around us — had constantly admonished us about all the terrible things "out there" that could get us.

"Don't cross the street."

"Don't go down the park."

"Don't play down The Dump."

"Don't! Don't! Don't! Or something truly terrible will happen to you."

(Through our pre-teens we were warned against playing near the railroad tracks because "Railroad Detective Campbell will get you, and you'll go to jail." For a decade, Detective Campbell was this very big authoritarian bogeyman. But when we got to high school, I was in the same class with Sheriff Neast's kid, and learned that another authoritarian figure, Sheriff Neast, was one of the nicest guys in the world. It would have been swell to go to the county jail. But that acquired wisdom came years later.)

So, anyway, the tonsillectomy pep talk had a hollow ring to it. Here were our parents, trying to convince us that we were going to have *fun* going to the Palmerton Hospital to have some people cut away our throats. I wanted to ask my parents if they'd had their tonsils out; maybe they'd join us and we could get a family rate. But even as a five-year-old, I could pick up the vibes that said, "Just shut up and resist in your own quiet way."

After days of being told we were going whether we liked it or not and resisting as best we could, we realized we were going to lose this one, so we fell back on negotiating the best deal we could get. We settled on the coin of the realm: comic books. If we each got a dozen comic books, preferably Scrooge McDuck, we'd acquiesce and have our throats sliced open. A sigh of relief issued from our parents, and then they told us that after the operation we could both eat as much ice cream as we wanted, as long as it didn't have any nuts or anything in it. Why they didn't throw that chip onto the negotiation table earlier, I don't know.

So they came back with a dozen comic books for each of us, stuffed our jammies into paper grocery bags (take that, Samsonite!), and hustled us off to the Palmerton Hospital.

They put us into a ward for eight people, but we were the only occupants. We'd arrived just before dinner time, and they threatened to feed us. Our parents vanished down one of the linoleumed corridors, leaving the same way they tell concerned children who have to put a parent with Alzheimer's into a nursing home to "Leave quickly and don't look back." The door closed on a spring, and Drew and I sat in our beds and looked at each other.

The foot of Drew's bed was pushed against a blank wall. Mine was as near to him as they could get it, but I had a bed with a view. I could look out a wide window down at a concrete walkway that ran beside the hospital; there were several trees overhanging and plenty of green grass and, beyond the little greenery, a parking lot. Drew looked at me and tears began to seep out of his eyes. Responsible to be the big brother, I put a big smile on my face and said, "What comics did you get?" He looked confused for a moment, not certain whether he should go ahead with the cry he wanted to pursue or respond to my question.

He pulled his paper grocery bag closer to him and dragged out a couple of the comic books Dorothy had stuffed in there. He held them up to show me the covers, one by one. Little Lulu. Casper. Despite the comic books, *I* wanted to cry. But I knew I couldn't afford to; I was Drew's big brother and I had to show some leadership here. Still, though, I felt like we'd been dumped into an orphanage — a very sanitary orphanage. I felt abandoned.

Drew became fascinated with his comic books and I listened to sounds coming through the closed door from the corridor and from the other side of the window. It was late enough in the afternoon that there must have been a shift change going on, because there was a half-hour or so of lots of activity on the walkway before it died down.

The uniformed woman who brought us our food on a tray seemed old, but was probably in her twenties. She was pleasant and asked us questions about why we were there. She asked Drew about his comic books, and then she left. We looked at our trays, uncertain what we were supposed to do with them. They had a curious, institutional smell to them, and everything seemed to be in miniature portions, not like we got at home. Drew balked; he didn't want to have anything to do with the stuff. I tentatively probed mine with a fork and began eating a bit here and there. It was pretty bland stuff. Drew followed suit and eventually we ate most of it.

When the lady came back to take the trays away, I asked about the ice cream we'd been promised. "Don't we get ice cream? My Mom said we'd get lots of ice cream." For a second, the lady looked confused. Then she smiled. "Well, of course you do," she said. "That's dessert. We save that for after you've eaten your meal. I'll be right back." Of course, nothing in a hospital happens right away. It took another twenty minutes or so, but she did return — with vanilla ice cream. Again, a miniature portion. We scoffed it up like turbocharged little vacuum cleaners.

Another woman came in and fluffed up our pillows and turned on a little night-light above the heads of our beds. We settled back to read comic books and shoot the breeze as men of leisure are wont to do. But we both knew we were playing the role of brave little soldiers. We were scared stiff — scared of the unknown. And, as it turned out, we had good reason to be.

After a fitful night watching strange shadows from the trees outside cavort on the wall above Drew's bed like so many silhouetted devils, we were awakened. Being the elder, I was taken first.

Lying on a gurney, all a kid sees is the ceiling going by. I don't remember much about the operating room except a handful of people wearing masks and talking soothingly, and one person, near my head, putting something over my mouth and nose that looked like the little strainer on the end of a handle — like the one Dorothy ran the gravy through to get the lumps out. There was a sharp odor — one of those smells I'll recognize for the rest of my life. And then I was gone — sort of.

Sooner than I was supposed to, I awoke. I awoke to find masked faces hovering over me and metal things — that from my perspective looked like shovel handles — coming out of my mouth. My eyes went wide and my mind attempted to send a scream to my mouth, but it was filled with fingers and metal devices — nothing worked. "He's awake!" someone said as someone else put pressure on my head to hold me still. There was some shuffling around as someone behind my head backed off, and then there was the gravy strainer again and the foul odor, and then I was groggily waking up back in the ward.

And Drew was gone.

I dozed off again and gradually came back up. There was a fuss at the door, and several medical people were bringing Drew into the room. I could tell by that telepathy kids have that there was something wrong; Drew looked dead. They laid him on the bed like a teddy bear minus the stuffing. (I don't know if I made this up later based on his subsequent problems or if it is a real memory, but I think there was a little spot of blood on the side of Drew's lip.)

For the rest of the day, they tried to staunch the blood seeping from the gouges in his throat — from which they'd stolen his perfectly good tonsils. People came in frequently to wipe the blood from his mouth and to look down his throat. When he did come to, he spent a lot of time whimpering. When the room was empty I tried to whisper to him to find out how he was doing, but he didn't seem to be capable of responding to my scratchy, harsh voice. He kept whimpering.

For the second time in his short life, he was looking down the long, dark, one-way tunnel, and from the sounds of it, he wasn't seeing a bright light and angels. As night came on, the staff was still hovering over him. They gave me some ice cream, which for the moment eased the feeling I had that someone had scrubbed my throat with steel wool.

My parents came by at one point and seemed concerned. They brought along more comic books and set them on the tray table between our beds, but the comic books remained unopened. I kept watching Drew. That night, when the demon shadows from outside the window began to dance on the wall above his head, I was scared they had come for him.

He still whimpered and tossed and turned. I kept calling to him softly in my croak of a voice, hoping to get a response. At one point he stopped thrashing and was quiet. In the light from outside, I could see him looking around as though he'd just come back from somewhere. He looked over and saw me and started to cry. Eventually he cried himself back to sleep.

I dozed off, too, and startled myself awake later when the nightmare began — a nightmare of metal tools coming out of my mouth, a regularly recurring nightmare that I'd have for years to come, always accompanied by that horrible smell.

In the aftermath of the tonsillectomy and waking under anesthesia, I developed a stuttering problem. This would be aggravated by a father who insisted that I stuttered to get attention (obviously, the last thing a stutterer wants), and intensified by the stress of going into first grade under the discipline of the Sisters of Christian Charity.

In my first-grade class at St. Joe's, we had thirty-seven students in the same room all day long under the guidance of the first-grade teacher, Sister Mary Friedeberta. As I recall, none of us had "attention deficit disorder," but four of the boys stuttered: Richie Guman, Catfish Gavornik, Bob Kmetz, and me. Richie and Catfish eventually "outgrew" it; Bob Kmetz and I didn't.

We four stutterers were all first-borns. In fact, thirty of the thirty-seven kids in our first-grade class were first-borns. I've often thought some sociologist or psychologist could have made tenure studying the dynamics of our class with so many first-borns in the wake of World War II.

But I digress.

Did I mention that I eventually married a nurse anesthetist? Is life a real pip — or what?

Hurricane One (Roof by Frisbee)

You can see the protective envelope that nature builds around kids by watching the way they sleep. Kids sleep the sleep of innocence — which is right next door to the sleep of death. You can pick them up by the ankles, transport them for miles on horseback, play Iron Butterfly records at full blast, and the only response you get from the little snoozers is a bit of drool. It was because of this deep sleep that I, at age six or seven, almost missed one of the most exciting events and profound disasters to ever hit 118 South Street, and I do mean *hit*.

When we went to bed that night, it was raining very hard; there was a fair amount of wind, too. But then, those are some of the absolutely best conditions for curling up under a warm blanket to go to sleep. I don't recall that there was any lightning that night, just wind: whistling wind, howling wind, wind with a mission — a mission beyond driving the rain horizontal.

Dorothy must have been shaking me for quite a while before I swam up to the surface from the deep sleep I'd been enjoying. There was a lot of noise and commotion up there on the surface, and it was dark; wind was howling much louder than it should have been allowed to, considering that we were inside a house. When Dorothy turned to try to wake Drew — who was even harder to rouse than I was — I wandered out into the hall and was surprised to see the attic door hanging open. And a lot of noise was coming down, as though there was a circus performing up there.

Curious, I climbed the steep, curving steps, surprised to feel wind and spray coming down the stairs. Instead of turning me around and sending me back downstairs where it was safe, it lured me upward. If my memory is clear on this point, I probably wore an expression not unlike the one the little kid in *Close Encounters of the Third Kind* wore when the alien spacecraft landed in his yard. Wonder. Awe.

Each step was more exciting for its anticipation of the unknown. (It registered only subliminally that I was walking, bare-footed, on steps that were wet.) As I reached the third step from the top, my head came above the level of the floor of the attic — the attic that had been, until that stormy night, used for storage. What I saw was riveting.

Shorty was engaged in a desperate wrestling match with a pair of bed sheets that were whipping around like a tag team of banshees. As they resisted mightily, he attempted to nail them to what was left of the roof. Rain was coming in all around him, from every angle — even from angles that defied gravity. Wind howled through the alleyway between our house and the Henritzys', louder than a runaway locomotive with the whistle tied down. Spikes of jagged wood, like angry teeth, surrounded the ragged maw of what had been the framework of the roof. The whole scene was lit eerily by the streetlight out front on South Street — a streetlight attached to a telephone pole that swayed drunkenly.

The combat in the attic looked like the cover of a men's adventure magazine — *True* or *Argosy* or *Saga*: a man risking his life against a charging elephant or a band of pirates or an advancing squad of Nazis. Shorty heroically battled elements that were gaining on him. I thought of Horatio Hornblower attempting to reef sails in the middle of a gale. But Shorty didn't yet have the upper hand; he was merely too stubborn to give in, attempting to force a thumb into a dike already breached.

The outside world was inside and the inside had been sucked outside. We had no roof on our house and nearly everything that had been stored in the attic had been sucked into the neighborhood. The roof was gone — vanished — and water, pushed stingingly by vicious winds, sprayed everywhere. The peaceful little town of East Mauch Chunk had been hit with a hurricane sent special delivery from the exotic lower latitudes of the Caribbean — Hurricane Hazel. Her magnificent winds had ripped the roof right off our house as though it were a candy wrapper, and sailed it away like the world's biggest Frisbee.

I stood transfixed for what seemed like hours (but was probably only a few seconds) before I was dragged down from behind by a frantic Dorothy, who feared I'd be stolen by the outlaw winds and sailed into the neighboring county, to be deposited in some other family's house. (Or perhaps she was determined to save me from my own adventures in Oz.)

Dorothy dragged me down the slick stairs, threw both of us into warm clothes, and trundled Drew and me downstairs, outside into the stinging rain, and down the street to the harbor of the House of Women. We were deposited there for safekeeping while she and Shorty and several of the neighbors worked for hours — hammering in boards and sheets and whatever they could lay their hands on to batten down the attic hatches against the storm.

Drew and I lay in adjoining beds whispering for what seemed like hours. I told him what I'd seen, careful to exaggerate nothing — that night, the adventure needed no exaggeration. We could hear the confirmation and reconfirmation of everything I was saying in the rain pounding at the window in our borrowed bedroom. Trees swayed and twisted outside like berserk skeletons. The wind howled and threatened, and we heard hushed, anxious voices outside our bedroom door.

By the time day arrived, the storm had moved on to harass other towns. The debris it left behind was tremendous. Tree branches, bed sheets, garbage cans, and newspapers were strewn everywhere. Dorothy was busy making sandwiches in our kitchen to feed all the neighbors who were busy hammering on a makeshift roof that would hold us over until a real roof could be mounted.

Later in the day, Dorothy took us for a walk to the lower end of South Street where it met First Street. There she pointed out to us a very bizarre sight: what had been our roof had sailed some one hundred yards down the street and had landed in the top of a big tree just inside the front yard of the Hermans' house — distant relations on my mother's side. (He was an insurance agent. Thank goodness.) The roof was bent and twisted as though a giant had crumpled and thrown away a big piece of aluminum foil. I don't remember how they got it down out of the tree; it must have been an enterprise worth studying.

There is nothing like a good, old-fashioned natural disaster to strike the ice pick of fear through the hearts of parents, or to provide the jolt of adrenaline that turns kids into little thrill junkies. "We must protect the children!" parents cry, while the children strain to break loose and take everything in. I share this incident of the hurricane that stole our roof because it was wonderfully unforgettable, the way such calamities are to naive little kids. It's the kind of frightening adventure that grown-up parents believe will traumatize their kids and make them grow up to need hundreds or thousands of dollars worth of therapy.

They forget that they were once kids, too. And they rolled with those punches just fine.

Hurricane Two
(A Truly Rocky Summer Camp)

In the summer following second grade (1954), an opportunity thrust itself upon some of us young squirts that seemed too dangerously good to be true. I naturally campaigned to capitalize on the opportunity to court danger and adventure.

St. Joseph's Parish owned a hunk of country land at the end of Germantown Road in a valley northeast of East Mauch Chunk, out by one of the town's reservoirs. Over the years, the land had been built into a summer retreat/camp called Our Lady of the Hills. The regal statue of Our Lady of the Hills occupied the highest point on the camp, save one. The outhouse, which was known fondly as Aunt Gussie, occupied a position in the woods just above Our Lady's statue.

Each June the camp was aired out and spruced up for day use, which consisted primarily of swimming in the cold spring waters that flowed into the cinder-block swimming pool. But for two very special weeks, the camp was sealed off from the outside world to be used exclusively by two overnight camping groups. The first week an army of boys invaded the camp to do what boys in the woods do: revert to the primitive. The following week, the place was turned into a camp for girls.

Physically, the property was open rolling fields surrounded by forest. The statue of Our Lady of the Hills occupied a grassy knoll that was the lower hip of Bear Mountain. A flagpole stood on the knoll with Our Lady. At the edges of the grass on both sides of the knoll, placed just inside the tree line, were a half-dozen wooden platforms upon which surplus, musky, moldy, mildewed army tents were erected for the weeks of camp. Each tent was named and each tent held roughly twenty kids. The higher up the hill your tent was placed, the higher your status.

The center of the camp was the main building, a squarish one-story place built into the hill below the tents on the north side, with a wide porch going around the lower two sides — one of which overlooked the rest of the property.

Below the porch was a crude basketball court (that only years later would be blacktopped). Below the court was the pool (which had to be drained and swept clean with stiff-bristled brooms every few weeks because the water was not chlorinated).

In the woods above the pool, there was a series of springs — whose temperature was approximately two degrees above the freezing point — that fed the pool with water. And below the woods to the north was what passed for the baseball field, which grew a tremendous bumper crop of rocks every winter so that every summer, for the first two days of camp, the entire army of kids used up several perfectly good hours each afternoon picking and transporting the rocks to the lower woods so that a mockery of baseball could be played there later in the week. (On that field, not even the best player in town could anticipate where a grounder was going to ricochet.)

Typically, the summer camp was attended only by kids who'd passed fourth grade. The kids who'd just graduated eighth grade were the camp counselors — terrorists who made life miserable for everyone younger. But for some reason — perhaps the still-persisting tales of the traumas visited upon the younger kids the previous summer — there were not enough takers to fill the ranks of lower castes for Summer Camp '54. In order to pay for itself, all of the beds had to be filled, so the assistant pastor lowered himself to the third graders, just before school let out, in order to cull some likely victims. Still, there were not enough sign-ups. So he moved into unprecedented territory — he canvassed the second-grade classroom.

Naturally, we little snot-nosed squirts, most of us trying to test everything and everyone in the vicinity, were elated. We were suddenly little big shots. We could hear the seventh and eighth graders grinding their teeth in disgust, certain that the neighborhood (Our Lady of the Hills) had gone straight to Hell, about to be overrun by a bunch of "babies." One eighth grader was heard to remark, "I signed up to be a counselor, not a damned babysitter!" (We duly noted who'd said it and placed him on the top of our hit list. He needn't have worried about "babysitting" us.)

The second grade was filled with the first wave of Baby Boomers, a decidedly ornery group; we could take care of ourselves, thank you very much.

Not too long ago I came across my second-grade First Holy Communion class photo from ol' St. Joe's. First of all, numbering thirty-seven in all, we were by far the largest class that had gone through the school to that point. And secondly, as I've said before, more than three-fourths of the holy smiling little faces were those of first-borns. That dynamic itself had a salutary effect upon the nature of our class.

We eight-year-olds rushed into the summer camp vacuum like a herd of rabid gerbils: Catfish Gavornik, Ron Hydro, my cousin Dave Herman, Eddie Moyer (whose family had years ago emigrated from French Canada), Freddie "Tree Toad" Armbruster, Richie Guman — even Charlie Bing.

To everyone else we were (naturally) the lepers, the lowest of the low, the slaves to everyone else — our main function: to provide punching bags for the rest of the camp. We were given the tent at the bottom of the hill (called — Ugh! — Blue Bell), which meant that when we had to go take a leak, our little legs had to carry us farthest uphill to visit Aunt Gussie. The tent was, naturally, the most moth-eaten of the lot, some of the floorboards were splintered and rotted, and they gave us the surplus army cots that were falling apart and smelled of eighth-level mildew and a dozen previous years of bedwetters. We didn't much care though. We were at camp!

We developed special pity for our counselor, for as counselor to the lowest caste of the low, he wasn't much higher. Every command sent downhill to our beleaguered counselor was meant as a degradation. But they'd overlooked one little matter: *we* didn't much care. *We* were at camp — several years earlier than expected. None of us cared . . . except for Charlie Bing. He cared.

We had no sooner unpacked our suitcases (and brown grocery bags) and stowed them under our cots on Sunday afternoon than our counselor was instructed to march us down to the "baseball field" to begin stone-picking. Get them young'uns broke in good — and fast! We made the obligatory grumbles and then marched off dutifully — all except Charlie Bing. He didn't move.

Charlie had apparently signed up for a week of relaxation away from his vexing younger brother Leo. Charlie's father had been a policeman who had died on the job — nothing as romantic as a shootout at a bank robbery gone bad; he'd just keeled over. Mrs. Bing doted on and spoiled Charlie and Leo. Mrs. Bing was a pleasant but always fretting, doughy woman whose wardrobe was stalled in 1942. She sent Charlie to camp with what appeared to us to be a crate of goodies: homemade cookies, Tastykake jelly-filled crumpets, licorice by the yard, a virtual candy shop of tooth-rotting stuff meant to keep her Charlie-boy happy — and fat.

Charlie didn't see his role at camp as a member of some chain gang doing ugly, sweaty work in the hot sun. This was either pretty dumb or pretty courageous of Charlie, since he was the kid in class everyone beat up. But that first day, he stood — or sat — his ground, and just plain refused to go.

Two counselors picked him up and carried him to the stonefield and sat him down on the ground. Charlie sat there with his arms folded across his chest, a little Buddha. When the counselors left, Charlie rolled to his feet and ran, as fast as a fat kid can, back to the tent. There, he lay himself down on top of his cot and pulled a cache of comic books out from somewhere under his bed.

This couldn't be allowed on the first day (and from the lowest of the low, no less). Two fresh counselors were sent to physically transport Charlie Bing to the work detail. He went kicking and screaming. They deposited him and once again he ran to his cot and lay down. This time four counselors walked into the tent and picked up the cot, with Charlie on it, and deposited him on the stonefield. His defiance was magnificent. We cleaned up rocks around him and tossed them into wheelbarrows and carted them to the lower woods.

Later in the day, one of the adult camp directors held a top secret meeting with the counselors and apparently laid down the law that they were to go easy on us eight-year-olds, being as how we were only babies and all. Riiiiiiight.

All week long we'd be the thorns in the sides of the older kids. We hadn't yet reached the age where we'd been civilized. We hadn't yet made the great leap from animals to human beings. Put us into a jungle or forest setting and we thrived. Any game or activity that involved physicality, we became feral.

(Years later, when I read *Lord of the Flies*, much of it resonated.)

Most of the counselors were post-eighth graders. They'd just recently graduated from St. Joseph's and many of them were in transition between grade school and seminary. On reflection, I guess there's nothing in this to be too surprised about, but, pretty consistently, those who were seminary-bound were the most sadistic of the counselors, never missing an opportunity to put a mean or punishing spin on anything that came to hand. You can't organize and pull off something like the Spanish Inquisition without good raw material, I suppose. And, to rationalize it, how could we as good Catholics expect our priests to be capable of consulting us on good and evil, and how could we expect them to know how to punish us for our sins, if they didn't already have (or develop) a bit of a proclivity in that direction?

Since it was a church camp, we were more regimented than a Special Forces unit. We did everything on the hour; we did everything together whether we wanted to or not. (We had only a half-hour to ourselves, that half-hour coming from 4:30 to 5:00 P.M.) At 5:00 we marched down to the main building, where picnic tables had been lined up along the porches, and we ate supper — unless we were on KP (kitchen patrol) that day, in which case we served supper and cleaned up afterwards. Of course we said our prayers before we ate, thanking God for what we were about to vacuum into our metabolically primed little bodies.

The food was plain but plentiful. The drink was what we referred to as *bug juice*, made with water and a sickeningly sweet Kool-Aid-like powder that they mixed in huge vats, into which they then dropped a block of ice — as though hyperactive kids needed even more sugar to make them act nuts. (Charlie Bing loved the bug juice — couldn't get enough of it.)

We called it bug juice because its astronomical sugar content drew bugs, all kinds of bugs, who then proceeded to drown ecstatically in the stuff. On the several occasions we conducted crude autopsies of the bugs under our plastic, cereal-box-prize microscopes, we could not determine if they'd drowned or been poisoned. In most of the flavors of bug juice it was easy to identify the bug corpses and pick them out, but every once in a while one would slip past our guard — especially if it was floating in the grape-colored juice — and it would contribute to our protein intake.

In the evening we would have story sessions of an uplifting variety on the hillside below Our Lady of the Hills statue. Our counselor would encourage us to tell stories after he got finished inflicting his on us; his were usually of a religious variety meant to elevate our minds and souls. Ours always involved severed limbs, giant gorillas, ghosts, and radioactive bugs that emerged from vats of bug juice.

At 8:00 P.M. precisely, the bell would be rung on the side of the main building for what was referred to as "canteen." As though we hadn't been fed enough sugar all day, we would line up and pick a specified amount of candy from a tantalizing display board. We were allowed (encouraged) to bring a dollar or so at the beginning of the week, and deposit it with the canteen. Then, each night at canteen, we were allowed to pick, for instance, five cents' worth of candy of our choice. This made certain that everyone was equal, everyone could buy exactly the same amount of candy, whether our families had lots of money or we were deliriously poor. Charlie Bing always complained that they were starving us to death by keeping the candy allotment way too low. (Why he complained, I don't know. He had his own illegal stash in his suitcase under his cot.)

Memory tells me it was Wednesday afternoon when the counselors helped the eight- and nine-year-olds move their cots onto the porches of the main building. They didn't tell us why. We learned later that the chief of police had come out to report that a hurricane was headed toward Pennsylvania and we should take all necessary precautions because it was going to hit us that night. And it did.

We little kids were in hog heaven getting to sleep on the roofed but open-sided porches. Our cots were lined up carefully, very Catholic, very military-like, and for a half-hour we whispered back and forth, occasionally receiving a command to "Keep it down out there!" as the adults slept on cots inside the building.

During the night, the winds picked up and the rain whipped around, but, like typical eight- and nine-year-olds, we slept through the best of it. We were later to learn that many of our parents, fearing the worst, drove out to check up on us, and I guess they were disappointed that we were not more concerned about what was going on around us. Catfish told us the next morning that he'd had to go pee during the night and got up . . . but was too scared to run off the porch and up the hill to visit Aunt Gussie, so he just peed over the side of the porch. (He got soaked when the winds blew his pee back at him.)

The entire camp was enlisted after breakfast to clean up the campgrounds, which were littered with fallen tree branches. It took us most of the morning to finish the job. In exchange for our selfless cooperation we were punished by being given an extra hour at the pool.

I say punished because each June, a week or two before camp started, the crews came out and drained the pool while brooming off the accumulated algae and scum that had built up on the walls all spring long. Then the pool was allowed to refill with water, diverted from the springs up in the woods. Since the spring water's temperature was roughly two degrees above polar ice, for the first half of the summer the pool was not the place anyone wanted to spend his time.

By August, the pool was wonderful and we could and would stay in it all day long. But in June, no way. The week after camp ended, the local doctors had a rash of visits by parents dragging their young boys in to have cases of undescended testicles checked out. It wasn't exactly that they hadn't descended, it was simply that when forced to make contact with that water they had run for cover.

The highlight of the week was Friday night, which was Ghost Night. Campers and counselors were not allowed to leave the grounds, but chaos was encouraged as the counselors chased campers around, attempting to roll us in a mud hole, dirty our faces with charcoal, cover our faces with melted lipstick, and do every unspeakable thing to us their filthy little minds could conceive.

But, at the gong of the mess bell at 8:00 P.M., everything was reversed. The counselors were then fair game for the campers and the campers were allowed — yeah, encouraged — to wreak vengeance on them. Most of the counselors were good sports about it, and we pounded the hell out of them for a few minutes. But, as in real life, the counselors we really wanted to get, the ones who deserved a pounding the most, those who'd been especially adept at sadism all week, were nowhere to be found. They'd all taken off for the woods and were hiding out, breaking the rules by leaving the grounds so they wouldn't get their just desserts.

But like most cowards who pick on those weaker than themselves, they weren't nearly as smart as they thought. They'd made the mistake of leaving all their belongings in their tents. You can guess the rest.

The Coal Man Cometh

Eventually, once the cellar of 118 South Street was cleared of ancient junk, Shorty laid a concrete floor and then built a cinderblock wall in anticipation of having a coal-fired boiler installed. The cinderblock wall closed off the whole front of the cellar (which retained its dirt floor) to form the coal bin, and a separate feeder bin was built off to the right. An iron "worm" or screw came out of the bottom of the smaller interior bin and fed coal through a pipe directly to the boiler. The front cellar window was hinged on top so it could be flipped back up inside the cellar so that when coal was delivered, a chute — down which the coal would flow — could be thrust through the window.

The boiler, all silver metal and pipes going in all directions, not unlike a Godzilla-sized cappuccino machine, squatted on the up-street side of the cellar floor, anchored with big bolts. A hot-water tank hung suspended from the ceiling with pipes running to and from the boiler — both sporting temperature gauges. It looked like the interior of a steam locomotive in miniature.

I don't recall the details of the installation. I may have still been living with Peter and Mary Herman. Shorty and the installers somehow got the monstrous thing into the basement without taking out a wall. Copper pipes went off to provide hot water to the new kitchen sink and the bathtub on the second floor rear, and a black pipe went to the hot-water radiators that had been installed throughout the house (except in the attic). We would no longer be warmed only by a coal stove in the kitchen, on which we'd had to heat water for washing dishes and bathing. We had suddenly gone ultra-modern, high-tech, state-of-the-art (if you lived in a backwater coal-burning part of the world). Some towns were on the verge of being served by nuclear power, while we had made the leap from coal stove to coal boiler.

The new boiler had two features from opposite ends of the technical spectrum. In the front of the boiler, sticking out of it like the stump of a lopped-off tree branch, was an opening to the infernal internal workings of the machine. On top of this coffee-cup-wide opening, a red metal cap was secured with screws that tightened it from the sides. In the middle of the red cap was a little metal door that you could flip up so that when the boiler was operating, you could stare into the fires of Hell. The hole gave visual access directly into the heart of the boiler, where coal that had once been prehistoric vegetation and dinosaur carrion was being slowly consumed by flame. The entire cap was removable because if the coal fire ever went out, you could access the interior of the furnace with a specially shaped coal shovel with a long handle with which you could insert some coal — after you'd pushed in some crumpled newspaper and some wood kindling to reignite the fire. It was a wonderment to take a piece of rag or a thick glove and flip up the hot little door and peer into the heart of heat.

At the other extreme, on the bottom of the boiler, was a door that swung out horizontally and was about the size of an access door on a Sherman tank. It was at ground level, and when you opened the door, you had access to . . . an ash bucket! This was the bane of our existence, for Drew and I were the ash bucket brigade!

For the entirety of our youth, Drew and I wrestled ash buckets filled with spent coal ashes up the narrow cellar stairs — pushing aside the winter coats that hung on hooks against the common wall with 116 South Street — lugged the ashes across the kitchen, and then trundled them down to The Dump. We had to monitor the buckets on a daily basis, because if we got behind and they overfilled, they could foul the grates, and that was a disaster. The coal would keep coming in through the worm and the flame would be smothered. After turning off the worm, we'd have to empty out the coal, mini-shovel by mini-shovel, and restart the fire — a laborious and lengthy process not unlike building the Suez Canal.

Coal — or more accurately, coal delivery — was the only matter of household economics to which we youngsters were ever exposed.

Every other Friday, when Shorty brought home his pay, a portion of it would be taken out and put away for the coal delivery in the fall. Everything would be budgeted around that event. Nobody was rich, so nobody on the street could afford to have a truckload of coal delivered and just whip out the cash and peel off hundred-dollar bills to pay for it.

The object was to amass at least enough cash to pay half the bill the day the coal arrived; the rest of the bill would be paid off on a biweekly basis through the winter months. Calls were made over the summer to check what the anticipated going rate for coal would be come September. Hence, the coal man became a banker for the neighborhood. The half-up-front would cover his costs for the coal down at the coal yard and the payments over the winter months would pay his "profits," which were eaten up with buying food, paying his mortgage, and paying the maintenance on the coal truck. The world of high finance flourished in our little neighborhood. I'm not sure why half the kids didn't go on to become financial wizards and Wall Street tycoons after the indoctrination they'd received at the altar of the Mason jar filled with cash for coal.

Ah, the coal truck. Ah, the coal man — er . . . sorry, Coal Man — in our case, a burly man named Jerry Cain who lived two blocks north of us in a corner house. No one in our neighborhood enjoyed a higher status or did his job with more verve and gusto.

The annual arrival of the Coal Man on the coal truck was a major neighborhood affair, when we could afford to own, certainly in a transitory way, a virtual mountain of coal in our own basement (in our case, seven tons of it), and when every kid from blocks around came to watch the ritual of its insertion into our house. And we reciprocated by eagerly attending the arrival of *their* annual coal order. (We were spoiled, though; our coal bin held seven tons, but the coal truck could only carry five tons at a time, so the Coal Man had to visit us twice.)

The Coal Man was to us kids a mythical figure nearly as high in the pantheon of heroes as Batman, The Flash, Richie Ashburn, or The Lone Ranger. When he arrived with a grinding of gears and a harassment of exhaust fumes, he expertly backed his dump truck up to the front of the house, avoided major tree branches, and tried not to roll the huge double sets of rear wheels over the hedge at the front of our little front yard — occasionally being forced to lay down planking to raise the downhill wheels (our section of South Street was on a definite dip toward the river) in order to adjust the attitude of the truck. The truck's bin was divided by four movable metal partitions; each of the five sections held a ton of coal. Coal came in various grades or sizes, gauged by the size of the chips. (We always ordered "pea" coal, but you could order all the way down to "rice.")

Once the Coal Man had his truck backed up precisely where he wanted it, he'd pull the chutes from under the truck's bin and hook together as many chute segments as he needed to reach the cellar window through which the coal would stream. And if the run was lengthy, he'd occasionally insert a brace under a segment of chute to keep it from buckling. He'd climb over and around and under his truck like a gorilla, covered all the time with black, greasy coal dust, fussing here and there with the truck — pulling this lever, making adjustments with that lever — until it was time for the fun to begin. The neighborhood kids milled about, their adrenaline coursing, getting in the way, being shooed away by the busy Coal Man and by the anxious mothers monitoring progress from their front windows.

The truck's motor would run on idle because once everything was set up to the Coal Man's satisfaction, he'd throw a lever and the hydraulic system under the truck's bed would begin to growl. The entire bin would rise on scissoring steel arms, the top of the bin brushing against tree branches and sometimes taking them with it, the truck's motor idling like a cat's purr one second and growling like a tiger the next — as the demands from the levitating tons of coal increased. The Coal Man would play the truck's levers like a baby grand's keyboard, adjusting the bin just right for maximum benefit from the laws of gravity. When the whole bin was high enough, he'd pull another lever and the front of the bin would rise even farther, creating a dangerous angle down which the coal was now eager to flow through the straining chutes.

At the back of the bin, low and in the center, was a metal door with a lever to raise it. Using a long metal rod with a hook on one end, the Coal Man reached up to the lever that controlled the little door and inserted the hook into the handle. "All right, you kids. Get back now. Get back," he'd growl at us in a low tone. The Coal Man never raised his voice. He possessed so much power over his disciples that he didn't need to resort to that to get results. No exclamation points were needed behind his orders.

We'd inch back, ready at the first rush of coal to retake the ground we'd lost by obeying the Coal Man's orders. He'd give a mighty yank on the handle end of the rod, the lever that raised the door would resist a bit, the Coal Man would swear under his breath — and each Coal Man had his own style of swearing, and each was noted, especially by our mothers, for the color of his swearing (and might lose some coal delivery business if ever he got to be too good at that). Finally, the Coal Man would wrench the handle just right, the door on the back of the bin would budge a little, sometimes open a half-inch or so, just enough to tease us with a little stream of water and coal.

But there was always that special moment when the resisting door would give, it would rise suddenly, and there was at first a roar and then a hiss of coal coming down the chute — a rush complete with an accompanying aroma of deep earth that filled the air like male perfume. The coal was watered down at the coal yard to make it slide more easily down the chute and in order to keep down the dust that would overpower everyone at the delivery site were it let loose unwetted. But even wetted, when stirred up by its rush into the chute, the aroma was overpowering.

The Coal Man would adjust the height of the door opening carefully, and with great skill. Open the door too much and the coal would come out too fast and flow over the sides of the chute. Open it too little and the Coal Man would be there all day waiting for the truck to empty.

While all this was happening, someone had to be in the basement coal bin. That person would use a shovel to push the coal around to dark corners of the bin, because if he didn't, the coal would form a pyramid which would (sometimes quite quickly) fill up to the end of the chute and back up the coal, causing the onrushing coal to spill over the sides of the chute and onto the lawn, where the individual coal peas made themselves very difficult to retrieve between the blades of grass.

It was our job — Drew's and mine — to go into the coal bin with shovels and move the coal around. Since Drew was left-handed, he took the "up" (120 South St.) side of the bin, while I took the "down" (116 South St.) side. Occasionally a calamity would occur, and when it did, the air surrounding the coal truck was punctured by white-hot curses and swearings that were wonderful for us kids to absorb. These would suck all the mothers on the block out of their houses to retrieve their children so their little ears wouldn't fall off and get transported directly to Hell (where they would burn in the eternal coal fire).

The Coal Man's visit was most exciting if you were splurging (as we were) and receiving more than a ton or two of coal. After the first ton went down the chute, the Coal Man would climb up the ladder on the side of the truck's bin, crawl into the bin, and unhook the next metal partition to let loose the next ton. The Coal Man wore high rubber boots and actually stood with his feet *in* the coal as it rushed for the open door.

If he was especially good at what he did, if he got the correct angle for the chute, if he opened the door just enough, and if the coal wranglers inside the cellar were moving the coal around fast enough, once he had everything set up, the Coal Man had no further duties but to lower himself into the truck's bin and walk around in the coal, urging the coal toward the open door and down the chute. Everything else happened by itself. The world of coal ballet was in perfect harmony. That was a performance that deserved a round of applause or two, or maybe even a standing ovation — the work of a well-seasoned maestro.

The Coal Man always had a dirty, beat-up old broom that, as the ton was nearly gone, he used to sweep errant coal out of the corners of the partition. He would then dismount the truck bin and use the broom to push any coal sticking to the chute down toward the waiting coal wrangler in the cellar so that the customer always received the full load.

When the coal had been successfully delivered, the Coal Man reversed the levers, and the huge scissor-arms lowered and the bin came back down to once again become a regular-looking truck instead of a dump truck. The last second of the process was the best, because as the bin lowered onto its metal guides, there was a tremendous metal-on-metal *clang*! The Coal Man slid his chutes under the bed of the truck, checked around for any loose pieces of equipment, and was off in a cloud of engine-exhaust fumes.

It was then our job to spend the next hour or two in the cellar redistributing the coal to the remote ends of the coal bin so it would be more even and at the same time easily accessible to shovel into the hopper where the metal worm inside the pipe would move it to the coal furnace as needed.

Nearly every week we'd want to be something else when we grew up: a cowboy (often), an Indian chief (occasionally), a miner (seldom), a railroad engineer (every night when the train whistles echoed up through the valley), a cop (only if we had a fast patrol car with a barrage of flashing lights), a fireman (during the Labor Day parade), or an astronaut (while reading a Tom Corbett, Space Ranger novel).

But on an annual basis, the week the Coal Man came rumbling down the street with the winter's supply of coal, every kid wanted to be a coal man (lower class — not *the* Coal Man; we knew we had to start at the bottom). And one year, in late August, after the Coal Man had made his delivery and all that was left of his visit was the acrid exhaust from his truck, a half-dozen of us decided that not only were we going to be coal men — we were going to be anthracite coal tycoons. That was the year we incorporated the White Coal & Navigation Company.

We named the company after Josiah White, who started the coal business in our area back in 1817. He founded the Lehigh Coal & Navigation Company, which shipped coal downriver to Easton and, from there, on to Philadelphia and New York. The coal went on barges through the canal he built along the Lehigh River. But we had a second reason for naming our company the White Coal & Navigation Company.

One of the major coal producers in the area shipped what was marketed as "blue coal." It was black coal like any other anthracite coal, but when they loaded it into railroad coal cars, they spray-painted blue across the top layer of coal. We'd always been fascinated by the long procession of blue coal cars that rumbled through town along the Lehigh Railroad tracks, and felt that we, too, needed a marketing gimmick. And it was easier for us to find some whitewash and a wide paintbrush than it would be to come up with any other color.

Our enterprising little group consisted of Raymond Otto from across the street, his younger brother Maurice (who ended up doing almost no work and who was later cashiered out of the company), one of the Franko kids, Junior Reis, Catfish Gavornik, and Patsy Bronko — the tomboy from up the street who was older than we were and who was good at bossing kids around. She was also good at regularly whupping us if we got the least bit uppity or didn't do what she told us to do.

Once we formed our company, our primary challenges were where to get coal and how to transport it once we got it. Our first meeting could be characterized as a meeting of the Junior Robber Barons. Patsy Bronko wanted to keep things simple: sneak into the coal yards after dark and steal coal, then resell it under our label. Contemplating spending the rest of our days locked up in the Carbon County Jail over on Broadway, where they'd once hung some Molly Maguires as domestic terrorists, we voted her down on that idea. (She didn't take the boardroom defeat very well.)

We finally settled on a two-pronged plan: pick fallen and discarded coal from along the railroad tracks as generations of poor folks had done, and also draw a map of all the places we knew of where a coal vein came to the surface — where we could pry chunks of coal directly out of the earth like real miners did. Once again, Patsy had her own nefarious twist: we should derail a train that was hauling coal; they'd come by to clean up most of the fallen coal, but they'd never bother to clean up all of it, so after they left, we'd swoop in with our little coal shovels and we'd be rich. Again, visions of our scrawny little bodies chained to the damp walls of the Carbon County Jail caused us to vote against Patsy's plan.

Her defeats at these meetings of the board of directors of the White Coal & Navigation Company were not going down well with her. She became moody and brooding and dark, and gave us the patented Patsy Bronko evil eye. We all (even the latent atheists among us) made the Sign of the Cross to ward off her evil look.

The second hurdle was transportation. I volunteered to dig out the old Radio Flyer wagon our mother had used to haul Drew and me up to the firehouse on Tenth Street to collect surplus food when our father was out of work. It was in serious need of repair, but we felt we were capable of bringing it back into service. We did this the next day, banging out dents, building taller sides out of discarded sheets of plywood (the better to hold in the coal), and painting it solid white, with "WC&N Co." written on both sides.

By day two of the White Coal & Navigation Company's existence, we were in business — sort of. We hauled the wagon down to the railroad tracks, and began dragging it along the service road that ran beside them. Unfortunately, we didn't find much waste coal. The newer, taller coal cars didn't leak coal like the old wood-sided cars used to. And the coal companies didn't fill the cars to overflowing as they once did, so there wasn't a great deal of coal that bounced out over uneven tracks or that pitched out when the cars went around a sharp curve.

Patsy Bronko didn't come with us. She was still pouting. But her idea of derailing a coal train started looking pretty good by 2:30 that afternoon when we stopped, while eating our peanut butter and marshmallow sandwiches, to assess our haul. We had a coffee can's worth of coal in the bottom of the wagon. We decided to abandon the railroad tracks and look to the exposed coal veins we'd mapped out.

We did a little better there, using screwdrivers and hammers to pry out hunks of coal. Much of the coal nearest the surface had already been picked over by the hobos who lived like trolls under the railroad bridges. With autumn coming on, they'd been out gathering as much coal as they could for their cool-weather fires before it became cold enough to send them transiting to Florida for the winter. Junior Reis, infected with the Patsy Bronko big-business philosophy, suggested we might raid the hobo camp and steal their coal. Although we'd occasionally sat with the hobos under the bridge while they drank their rank coffee, and found them to be good enough company with terrific stories to tell, we decided that if they ever caught us stealing the coal they'd mined, we'd be dead meat — our bodies rotting, hung up on tree branches sweeping the top of the nearby river.

We didn't wear watches, but could tell it was time to go home for supper when the volume of traffic rattling over the bridge increased, indicating that our fathers were coming home from work and that we'd better do the same. We didn't want to haul such a meager load of coal up River Street, so we stowed the coal wagon and tools inside a big drainage pipe that emptied into the river. It took only three of us to lift the wagon into the pipe, our haul was so meager. We trooped off to supper and promised to be out good and early the next day to continue digging up the black diamonds. And we were.

By the end of the second day, we had a good eighteen inches of coal of various sizes piled in the wagon. The plywood sides were not in any danger of collapsing under the load. Over our mid-afternoon lunch, we concluded that we'd need to crush the bigger pieces of coal in order to sell it in our neighborhood, because very few people still had coal stoves — where it didn't matter much what size hunk of coal you put in, just as long as the stove was fired up. (In fact, with the coal stoves, the bigger the chunk, the longer it burned.)

Most people had changed over to the coal boilers, which required a consistent size of coal — usually a very small size so it could be effectively pulled through the pipe with the coiled metal worm inside. Heck. Some of the people had actually turned traitor and had converted to heating oil!

So we set to work hammering the coal chunks down into more manageable sizes. (Many years later, on a trip to India, I watched women squatting at the side of the road hammering big rocks into little rocks to be used in road building and repair. It didn't strike me as much of an alien occupation — as it *had* struck most of the tourists in our group, who were from non-coal-producing parts of the country.) By the end of the day, Maurice Otto had resigned his seat on the board of directors, and he went off to loaf somewhere. Patsy still had not returned to reclaim her leadership role, so we were down to just five collier-tycoons.

We slowly lumbered up River Street, taking turns hauling the wagon behind us. We couldn't go through the park because there was no way to drag the wagon up the numerous steps. When we reached South Street, we parked the now grit-covered white wagon in our backyard, determined to paint the coal white tomorrow before making our first big sale. We'd then reinvest the money in the company by buying bigger and better tools with which we could pry the hard coal from the harder ground.

Fortunately, none of our parents learned of our enterprise, or they'd have had our hides, because the last thing parents on our street wanted was for us to "bother the neighbors." Bothering the neighbors was restricted to three times a year: selling Easter candy, selling Christmas cards, and trick-or-treating for Halloween. Our parents knew nothing of what was afoot, other than that we'd once again found something to occupy our time — and, as a result, we were staying out of their hair. For all they knew, the world was in perfect balance.

The next morning we were up early, prying the lid off the gallon can of whitewash. We'd already used nearly half the can ineptly splattering white onto our wagon — er . . . coal truck. The absurdity of painting a coal truck white was only now beginning to sink in. The white sides of the wagon had become grayed as we'd pursued our profession. Raymond suggested we repaint the wagon before putting a white layer over the top of the coal but we voted him down. We didn't have enough whitewash for both jobs.

We slathered the whitewash onto the top of our coal. In retrospect, I can see it was not a good idea to use a brush. The brush absorbed more coal dust from the surface of the coal than it put down white on top of it. The coal became an off-white and then a gray. The brush wasn't working, but we could see no better alternative. Junior suggested we sprinkle whitewash *atop* the coal to avoid mixing it *with* the coal. We tried that and quickly used up the rest of the can. In the end, our coal looked very much like a pile of white chocolate Raisinettes.

A gradual resignation to the sorry state of our coal's appearance overcame us, and we trudged off down beside the house and out onto the sidewalk. We headed uphill first, figuring that by the time we were tired we'd have gravity on our side to bring us home.

We skipped the Henritzys and moved on. Nobody home in the next house. The Derkoshes laughed at us and closed the door. Nobody home at the Barachys. The next house belonged to Raymond's uncle; he laughed at us and wished us good luck. And so it went. Selling something everyone needs wasn't easy. How could people sell folks stuff that they didn't need when we couldn't even sell the essentials of life? Nobody to that point had even asked us what we were charging for the load. We had discussed that the day before; we were charging a dollar.

We had no luck all the way up the right side of the block. We diplomatically skipped Patsy Bronko's house. Then we had a brilliant idea. We'd try Mrs. Hefferling. She lived two houses over on Second Street and she still had a coal stove in her kitchen. You could occasionally see her coal bucket sitting beside the side door to the kitchen, under the porch overhang.

Mrs. Hefferling was probably the oldest lady within a block. She was a Norman-Rockwell-type old lady, all smiles and pink and friendly. Her one shortcoming was that at Halloween she made us recite twenty-four stanzas of "Frog Went A-Courtin'" in exchange for a crummy apple. She didn't believe kids should have candy. It would rot their teeth and spoil their brains. She was one of the only people within a block who regularly drank tea, which she took with a teaspoon of honey. She was obviously a bohemian.

The four of us rolled toward her kitchen door. We could see her sitting in her kitchen sipping tea from a delicate teacup. She saw us coming and got up to meet us at the door.

"My," she said. "Is it Halloween already?" She smiled a smile that told us she was (of course) playing with us. Besides which, it was only 9:15 in the morning and we weren't wearing costumes.

"No, Ma'am," Junior said. "We're sellin' coal. So people can stay warm over the winter."

"I see. But what happened to it?" Mrs. Hefferling asked. "It's painted..."

"White," I said. "Because we're the White Coal & Navigation Company."

"Like blue coal—only white," Raymond added.

"Like... sort of white," the Franko kid said. I elbowed him in the ribs to keep him quiet. (It's not good business to disparage your own company and its products.)

"White," I said again, unnecessarily. "Like Josiah White."

"Will it still burn—with white paint on it?" Mrs. Hefferling asked.

To be honest, we had no idea. "Sure it will," Raymond said. "White coal burns just as good as blue coal." He nodded in satisfaction at his own scientific knowledge. "Even better," he added for good measure. "Cleaner, even."

"Because it's more pure," Junior added.

(Our sales skills were quadrupling by the minute.)

"And it's hand-picked," I added, as though I were selling strawberries.

Mrs. Hefferling smiled. "I used to pick coal down along the railroad tracks when I was a girl. We couldn't afford to buy coal then." Her eyes wandered off and she stared into the sky for a moment, probably picturing herself picking coal. She smiled to herself as though she enjoyed picking coal. (We sure hadn't been smiling when we were doing it, but I guess that's the difference between working and reminiscing.)

"How much does this wonderful load of white coal cost?" Mrs. Hefferling finally asked after she'd returned to Earth.

Not one of us was ever going to make it big in sales. "Sixty-nine cents!" Raymond blurted. I nearly hit myself on the head with the palm of my hand. Sixty-nine cents! (Raymond somehow knew the number "69" was nasty, but it would be another two years before he found out why.)

Mrs. Hefferling blinked twice at the "sixty-nine," then looked taken aback, startled. She recovered when she realized Raymond didn't have any idea what he was talking about. "Sixty-nine cents. For world-famous white coal. Why, I never."

"We could do it on the layaway plan," Junior piped up.

"No, no," Mrs. Hefferling said. "Take it over there" — she pointed to a little wooden coal bin that sat against the side of the house — "and begin to unload it and I'll get your money."

She backed into the kitchen, leaving the door open.

Before she could change her mind, we hustled the wagon down the walkway and began shoveling the coal into her bin. In less than five minutes we were finished. Of course we'd never thought to wet the coal down to hold down the coal dust. Our white wagon was in serious need of a hose — and so were we.

Mrs. Hefferling was waiting for us. She counted out five dimes, three nickels, and four pennies. We dutifully tipped our hats and backed out of the walkway. "Don't forget to come back for trick-or-treat," she said. "I'll have some really delicious apples waiting for you."

"Yes, Ma'am," Junior said.

We dragged our now-lightweight wagon to the corner and I held out my hand with the coins in a big pile.

"Hey, we were charging a buck," the Franko kid said.

"Special price to widows," Raymond said.

"Yeah," Junior said. "Widows ain't got much money."

As we stood there looking at the loot, we held an impromptu board meeting — as it would turn out, our last board meeting. Bernie Leinhart's grocery store was a mere two blocks away, over Second Street and down Center, and the bottom shelf of his display case was chock-full of penny candy.

Junior wanted to buy tools like we said we were going to so we could do more mining and thereby enlarge the company. "What kinda crappy tools can we buy with sixty-nine cents?" the Franko kid said. He was right. And so we voted. We voted to dissolve the White Coal & Navigation Company right there. We'd be going back to school in a week or two anyway, and this coal mining was hard work. Maybe not as hard as *selling* coal, but our company covered both ends of the business, so we decided it was just too much for us.

In the end we voted to give Maurice Otto and Patsy Bronko five cents each as their share, and the five of us who'd stuck it out each got a dime — which, over the next several days, we frittered away on Mary Janes, Bazooka gum, B-B-Bats, Bit-O-Honeys, Dots, and other delectable cavity fertilizers. We voted to give the nine cents to my father to repay him for the whitewash we'd used. That night, I snuck it into the Mason jar. They remained the only coins in the jar for the next year; Dorothy and Shorty never questioned their origin. We rolled the wagon back behind the house where it could spend the winter getting rained and snowed on — which action, thank goodness, virtually erased the dreadful whitewash job.

Little by little, over the next few years, fewer and fewer people sported signs in their front windows that proudly declared "We Burn Coal." The Coal Man eventually fell onto hard times and even *he* converted to fuel oil. But wrestling a big old python-like hose from the tanker truck at the curb to a fitting in the side of the house just isn't the same as opening that little door in the back of the coal truck to let loose the rush of musty pea coal.

It took our family a long time to convert from coal to fuel oil. In fact, it didn't happen until I was away at college — or perhaps later. So, for years, Drew and I lugged ash cans, filled with the detritus of coal heating, up the cellar steps, across the kitchen floor, and down the backyard — and dumped them at the edge of The Dump. Once or twice a month Drew or I would take a metal rake down and smooth out the ash heaps. And, little by little, The Dump vanished under the ashes.

I'm sure there's some great symbolism there, beyond the texture of the neighborhood changing under the rolling tank wheels of progress. Progress eventually seeks us out and changes our lives, whether we want it to nor not. We are powerless in its grasp; we can resist for a while, but eventually it wins. Always. And it's often a matter of geography as to how long it takes progress to seek us out, find us, and alter us forever.

Jim Thorpe Never Slept Here

The nest in which we are hatched and away from which we eventually take flight enfolds us forever like an invisible topcoat. Of course, as anyone who's gone through the bargain basement of a Salvation Army store knows, topcoats come in many designs and in an infinite variety of cloths and are most famously worn by film noir detectives and sexual perverts.

But let's discard the mixed metaphor of nest and topcoat and, instead, consider a house under construction. Genetics set the human parameters — in the analogy of the house, the foundation and frame. Environmental forces (place and parents, but even more than parents, siblings — or lack of same — and friends) determine the roof and walls. Imagination furnishes and decorates the inside, and a mixture of genetically induced and peer-pressured habits splash paint on the outside. Our acquired eccentricities do the landscaping. Mansion or single-wide, money plays no role.

There. Fifty thousand years of human evolution and development distilled into one paragraph, and the price is whatever the publisher affixes to the back of this book. A printed diploma costs extra. A CD-ROM is just plain overkill.

We would execute a whole forest of trees to wrest the necessary pulp to make paper to print the thousand-plus-page book we could write on the importance of *place* in great literature. What self-respecting Russian novel works without it? *Crime and Punishment* reverberates with evil, and what makes evil drip its venom *is* the claustrophobic warrens and alleys in which the action — both emotional and physical — takes place. Would *Crime and Punishment* work as well at Furnace Creek in Death Valley? In an Eskimo village? On a tropical island?

And in the French, what is *Germinal* without the dank close quarters of the coal mine? Would it work on a mountaintop? What a meager impact *The Adventures of Huckleberry Finn* would have if we removed the river. And the forest we cut down to make the paper for our million-word treatise on *place* is at this very moment forming and deforming the character of those folks who live along its edges or who wander through it.

I have long harbored grave concerns about the influence of the place where others (and I, myself) raised me; it was such a schizophrenic place. At one time it wallowed in wealth, then it became incredibly poor, then it reinvented itself. At one time its identity was determined by the transportation of anthracite coal; now it depends largely on the transportation of tourists within its borders. On one side of the river the town sprawls, while on the other side it is cramped by ancient mountains. It at one time went so far as to boast competing railroads on either side of the river.

And then there are the names. Where most towns are content with one name, our town used up two and was on its third when I grew up. There was even a movement, half-serious, to move on to a fourth.

Since 1816, the cramped side of town was called Mauch Chunk; the sprawling side of town across the river was East Mauch Chunk. In 1954 the two sides joined and called themselves Jim Thorpe, and in the 1960s, after JFK's assassination, a move was afoot to change the name to Kennedyville. (There is no evidence that either Jim Thorpe or John Fitzgerald Kennedy ever visited Mauch Chunk or even heard of it. Why would they? From the outside world, Mauch Chunk wasn't easy to get to — which had its positive side for those who lived there.) With the usual adaptive creativity of most kids, we referred to our new conjoined town as Jim Chunk — only because it sounded better than Mauch Thorpe.

Jim Chunk is the county seat of Carbon County, Pennsylvania. It is located in the central-eastern section of Pennsylvania, roughly halfway between Allentown/Bethlehem and Scranton/Wilkes-Barre, neither of which, that I know of, ever contemplated joining their twin towns into one.

The town is surrounded by the worn-down Appalachian Mountains and is cut in two by the Lehigh River, which takes a dramatic curve around Bear Mountain on the east. As I've said, Bear Mountain was named Mauch Chunk by the Leni Lenape Indians, because to them it resembled a sleeping or reclining bear. (The Leni Lenape are the same Indians Ben Franklin refers to in his autobiography: "The Indians had burned Gnadenhut [later Lehighton, four miles from Mauch Chunk], a village settled by the Moravians, and massacred the inhabitants." They apparently had a great deal of spare time on their hands to indulge their imaginations between burning villages.)

In its heyday, Mauch Chunk, so the local lore goes, was home to more millionaires (eleven) than inhabited New York City. This was in the second half of the nineteenth century. The town's wealth came from its perch on the river, from whence it could ship anthracite coal and lumber (by rail and canal barge) to major metropolitan centers.

Mauch Chunk was blessed by its location on the river and by the fact that it harbored very little coal itself. It positioned itself at the eastern extreme of the coal-rich mountains on which grew the towns of Lansford, Coaldale, Summit Hill, Nesquehoning, Tamaqua, etc. — towns that undercut themselves with deep mines and scarred themselves with surface ("strip") mines. The object of their efforts was to send more and more coal to the coal and transportation barons in Mauch Chunk so *they* could, in turn, repackage it and ship it downriver to Philadelphia and New York City — while *their* town remained relatively unscathed by the violence of separating the riches from the earth.

The virgin forests surrounding Mauch Chunk were clear-cut to provide shoring for the deep mines and to build canal barges. The barges were filled with coal and eased down a series of locks. They eventually arrived at Easton, where the coal was unloaded and sold, and the barges were broken up and sold as lumber. There are, no doubt, a few older houses in Easton built with lumber from the mountainsides around Mauch Chunk — some of it from Bear Mountain itself. We can only hope that people sleeping in bedrooms made from Bear Mountain lumber sleep as well as does the slumbering bear above Jim Chunk.

Physically, Mauch Chunk/East Mauch Chunk was a lovely place, as long as you didn't look too closely. In the 1950s, from a perch on Big Rock on the top of Bear Mountain, a kid could survey the very distinct and separate sections of the town(s).

As the Lehigh River reached the towns — with railroad tracks bordering it on both sides, Lehigh Valley on the east side, Jersey Central on the west — it took a sharp forceful turn around Bear Mountain. East Mauch Chunk sprawled, just before the inside of the turn began, stretching itself along the ancient alluvial fan created by eons of rain and wind wearing down the eastern mountains. On the outside of the beginning of the river's curve — a curve caused by the precipitous mountainside that the river's patient sculpting had not been able to undermine — lay Mauch Chunk, poured into a side valley notched perpendicular to the river. Broadway meandered up the narrow notch, eventually expanding to a farmland valley as it rose beyond the notch.

If you stand at the bottom of Broadway and look up and to the right, your eyes meet the stately Asa Packer Mansion perched on a steep hillside. If you walk up the steep hillside, you reach a ridge-line onto which clings the third section of Mauch Chunk, known as The Heights. At some point before the nineteenth century wore itself out, someone designated Mauch Chunk, "The Switzerland of America." The town had serious hopes that its vaunted history, its natural beauty, and its small-town charm would earn it a niche as a tourist mecca. That has since occurred, but not without pain, and — here's the irony — not without resistance from a large segment of the population that would have been helped by such a turn of events.

I should pause here and sate the reader's curiosity concerning the town's name change, which occurred amidst great controversy and fanfare in 1954. It is a story fraught with the naïve big-time dreams of small-town America.

These days, small towns (and some large towns that have fallen on hard times) are ripe for being bludgeoned into submission by the promise of economic rebirth through the miracle of theme-park-like gambling schemes. Mauch Chunk and East Mauch Chunk were cajoled and conned into being dragged into the twentieth century by the promises of riches and fame. These would supposedly accrue to our town if it became the final resting place of a famous dead Indian's homeless remains.

Prior to 1954, Mauch Chunk (including The Heights) and East Mauch Chunk were two separate and distinct towns, conveniently separated by the river. Each town had its own mayor, town council, police force, etc. Combined, the towns boasted a population of five thousand. Since the demise of King Coal, neither town was doing well. There had been occasional talk of the towns joining in order to save money on duplicated municipal services, but there was a great deal of rivalry and ego that got in the way, a great deal of jockeying back and forth to see which side would get the upper hand in such a deal. In such things there is *always* an upper hand, and if there is an upper hand, there must also be a lower hand — a raw deal nobody wanted to be stuck with. In the meantime, the duplication of services made the poor little towns ever poorer.

The widow of Jim Thorpe — the great Indian athlete and, arguably, the greatest athlete in the history of the world — was making the rounds of Oklahoma towns in a desperate attempt to find a final resting place for poor Jim. Unfortunately, besides having been stripped of his Olympic gold medals because he had accepted some expense money while playing ball one summer, Thorpe had sunk so low late in his career that he'd done a stint as a professional wrestler in an attempt to make a living. (Obviously, he was decades ahead of the curve on that one.) He had ultimately drunk himself to death and had thereby turned himself from a legend into a disgrace. No self-respecting Indian town in Oklahoma, the state of Thorpe's birth and childhood, wanted anything to do with their wayward son. The Sac and Fox tribes disowned him.

When Mrs. Thorpe ran out of prospects in Oklahoma, she turned to Pennsylvania. Thorpe had gone to the Indian school in Carlisle in south-central Pennsylvania. But Carlisle didn't want to make space for Thorpe's by now train-trip-lagged body to lay itself down for some much needed rest at his alma mater.

Still hoping to connect with a town with an Indian history, Mrs. Thorpe turned to the twin Mauch Chunks. She had heard of the towns' brave attempts to sidestep ruin by collecting a nickel a week from local families in an attempt to begin an economic development fund. Mrs. Thorpe rolled into the towns and struck coal dirt. By this time, she had sharpened her spiel on enough prospective sites that it was keen-edged.

In the Mauch Chunks, she began carving away at the skepticism, cynicism, and plain stubbornness of the movers, the shakers, and the ne'er-do-wells in these towns named after a mountain that supposedly looked like a sleeping bear. Her pitch was simple but eloquent in that it promised just what many of the people in the Mauch Chunks had been waiting for: a hero on a white horse (or, in this case, probably a pinto) to save it — even if being saved was to come by way of a dead Indian and not the cavalry.

The pitch was this: If you good folks rename your towns Jim Thorpe in honor of my husband, your lovely little combined towns will be on the map. Your new town will be mobbed by businesses that want to be associated with the world-renowned reputation of Jim Thorpe. There will be a two-hundred-bed hospital. There will be manufacturing plants that will employ everyone for miles around who wants a job, so no breadwinner will ever again have to commute thirty miles, one way, to make his bread. Your real estate holdings will soar in value. And on, and on, and on. (The response at some of the local watering holes was this: "We already got all the drunks we need.")

But Mrs. Thorpe took her pitch to the high and the mighty. One of the highest and mightiest to receive the call was Joe Boyle, editor and co-publisher of the Mauch Chunk *Times News*. Joe was one of the town's most active boosters and one of the region's most colorful characters. Joe began on a daily basis to promote the idea of joining together that which nature had separated by a river. The newspaper was filled with it. And Joe was willing to go to any group and talk about the prospect of joining the Siamese twins. He found followers. The momentum grew.

Joe's group had already put together the Nickel-a-Week Foundation. Every Saturday, the knock would come on the door, the hand would be extended, the screen door would open a crack, and the requisite nickel would be deposited, with the deposit being duly noted in a little book. (Maybe the towns should have become Nickel, Pennsylvania.) Meanwhile, the lawyers were stirred up on both sides of the river, and they began examining and probing and exploring the legal implications of joining the two towns, while the mayors said things in speeches that would contribute to their being elected as the first mayor of Jim Thorpe, Pennsylvania, the phoenix towns. (Maybe the towns should have become Phoenix, Pennsylvania.) Of course, there were lots of discussions with the state about who would get to pay for all the new highway signs that would help the hordes of investors and wannabe citizens find Jim Thorpe amidst the bucolic mountains and valleys.

When the vote finally came down, the proposition of joining the two towns into one passed, but barely. Change is not a welcome visitor in most parts of Pennsylvania, even today. The town whipped itself into a frenzy as time came for the actual marriage. Parades were organized, speeches were constructed, and there were even soapbox derbies on the impressively steep Fisher's Hill on Center Street in East Mauch Chunk.

Street signs were changed while newspaper photographers recorded the event. Some businesses changed their names from Mauch Chunk–this or Mauch Chunk–that to Jim Thorpe–this or Jim Thorpe–that — but others didn't. The police force was reorganized, and it was hoped that much of the borough's redundancy could be phased out as soon as possible. But there was no big rush now that the joining had been approved. The fact that the deed had been legally consummated was enough for a lot of folks.

Everyone sat back and waited eagerly for the onslaught of prosperity.

And then they waited some more.

Then they even waited more than that.

And nothing happened.

There was a rumor that Joe Boyle had run off with the funds from the Nickel-a-Week program — which was ridiculous, since people could daily see Joe running around town chasing down this or that fast-breaking story for his newspaper.

But nothing happened — other than people in other towns continuing to laugh at Jim Thorpe, Pennsylvania.

Eventually, a plot of land was purchased (with Nickel-a-Week funds) on the upper edge of what had been East Mauch Chunk. The plot was originally intended as the site of either the manufacturing plant or the hospital, I forget which. But when neither was forthcoming, it was made the site of the official Jim Thorpe Mausoleum, in which would be interred the mortal remains of the great Indian athlete — which Mrs. Thorpe was obliged to provide.

Of course, the mausoleum wasn't yet completed, so while the work went on, Jim Thorpe's body was held in custody at one of the town's cemeteries. And now that some of the naïve fervor had subsided, some of the ringleaders wanted to go to the holding cemetery and view the corpse of Jim Thorpe. Aware that they had led the two boroughs down an uncertain path, they wanted to be certain they had, at least on this point, gotten what they'd bargained for. Joe Boyle would subsequently tell and retell the story of what they found when the lid was raised, and he was seldom forced to exaggerate more than a little bit during the telling of the story:

The committee reverently stood before a casket. The undertaker raised the lid. Inside, a corpse was wrapped in a body-sized clear plastic bag, the body stiff and wizened, but very evidently the body, in all its detail, of Jim Thorpe, the greatest athlete the world had ever known. And, since Joe Boyle was a journalist — and an ardent sports fan to boot — everyone has, for decades, taken his word for that. Jim Thorpe is indeed buried in Jim Thorpe.

What made it even more apparent that the town had the real Jim Thorpe was that, some years back, Thorpe's tribe in Oklahoma changed their attitude concerning the legacy of Mr. Thorpe and attempted to wrest the body from the good people of Jim Thorpe, Pennsylvania. But Jim Thorpe, the borough, fought and won the battle to keep him. Possession is nine-tenths of the law. Once again, the Indians were defeated.

But the foibles of people are not limited by the color of their skin. When he died in 1953, Jim Thorpe's people in Oklahoma didn't want to have anything to do with him; the people in the Mauch Chunks were "taken in" to the point that they did. And when the folks in Oklahoma were sufficiently over their embarrassment, they changed their minds. I want to suggest that the entire process closely joins Jim Thorpe's family and tribe with the tribe of residents of Jim Thorpe, Pennsylvania. This is how:

When I graduated from college in 1968, I returned to the Jim Thorpe area to work as managing editor of the paper Joe Boyle had been editing. (In fact, Joe Boyle hired me right out of college and then proceeded to resign from the paper a week before I started work on it, but that's a story for another time.) I worked on the newspaper for four and a half years. During that time the seeds of a fledgling tourist trade had been rustled up. Years later, when I returned to town for a visit, I found that the tourist trade had indeed taken root.

Outsiders from Philadelphia and New York responded to the tourist bureau's efforts and came to Jim Thorpe to visit, fell in love with the town's historic and natural charms, and returned to buy property, fix it up, open shops, and prosper while serving, or feeding upon (whichever term you care to apply) the tourist trade.

The first response of many of the residents of Jim Thorpe was that all these damned outsiders were coming into town and ripping us off. As is the case with human nature, the locals who complained the most and loudest were those who had, in the past, done the least to improve the town and its reputation.

Race Street, which consisted of several blocks of very European-style stone row homes with the back wall built into the side of the mountain one street off Broadway, had fallen into advanced stages of decrepitude. If Jim Thorpe needed a ghetto, Race Street was eager to skulk forth to qualify. The row homes were still sturdy, but most were in need of infusions of cash and tons of tender loving care. One of the units stood gutted, as though it had been the target of an Allied bombing in World War II. In 1968, when I returned to town to work on the newspaper, that particular piece of real estate had been on the market for several years with no takers. The asking price was $800.

Most residents of Jim Thorpe were either indifferent or outright hostile to the idea of their town becoming a tourist destination. They resisted the resurrection of the town with more vigor than they'd ever expended on improving it. And when the outsiders from New York and Philadelphia moved in and bought some of the row homes on Race Street, poured tens of thousands of dollars into them, turned them into shops, and began reviving the town, there was a narrow-minded antagonism toward them. One lifelong resident claimed that natives should have gotten first crack at the houses on Race Street. When I reminded him that he could have bought one of the row homes for $800 any time he wanted, the conversation rapidly degenerated.

So it is in that context that I view the defeat of Jim Thorpe's relatives in Oklahoma to reclaim a body they had shunned in 1954. They are merely different colored patches in the quilt of human nature, as are the residents of Jim Thorpe who failed to buy the homes on Race Street and then complained loudly and often when someone else did.

As far as the Indian legacy of Jim Thorpe (the town) goes, there were two watersheds: the original Leni Lenape Indians who, in a slouching, tired Appalachian mountain, saw a sleeping bear; and the kids of European immigrants who grew up there whose parents referred to them as little Indians — kids formed by the natural contours of the town and surrounding mountains perhaps more than they were by their own parents and grandparents.

In much the way the Mississippi shaped Sam Clemens, Mauch Chunk shaped the kids who ventured outdoors to experience it. Confined by parents who believed in disciplining their kids on a regular basis, the kids responded to the physical nature of the region that encouraged wildness. The Lehigh River, the ruins of the canal locks, Bear Mountain, railroad tracks on both sides of the river, old mine shafts, and a thousand nooks and crannies gave the area an infinity of adventures waiting to be uncorked.

The town had profited from the coal in the previous century, but had not been scarred by it as had other coal towns. What scarring had been done had been the building of the railroads and the construction of the canal locks. The former was in decline by the time I was born; the latter hadn't been in use for over a decade. But the remnants were like abandoned castle walls — from a legendary era — within which a kid's imagination could blossom on a languid summer day. The grownups talked about the legendary era, about the eleven millionaires, the thousands of summer visitors, and the nine hotels. We, the kids, regularly found ruins — to us, not unlike Stonehenge — that proved the legends had a basis. Big Rock at the peak of Bear Mountain, a huge mass of conglomerate stone, was our Walden Pond. Along the river, there were cool tunnels and walled-up cellars that had long been abandoned but that we reopened.

But we didn't have a monopoly on the dark places. The 1950s marked the end of the hobo era, when men who'd chosen to live the wanderer's life gathered under the railroad trestles to sleep and cook their food and brew their strong coffee in the cans it came in. They would occasionally wander into town to knock on a door to inquire if they could do some odd jobs in exchange for soup and a sandwich and some spare change. Our parents would have locked us in the cellar to rot away if they'd known we spent many a contented hour sitting around the friendly hobo fires listening to stories of faraway places and dreaming of someday seeing what *they'd* seen.

We loved the adventure of accidentally wandering onto railroad property — which was difficult to avoid considering there was so much of it — which was further enhanced by the constant threat of being arrested by Special Railroad Detective Campbell, who reputedly lived for nothing nobler than to catch and prosecute kids bold enough to have their fun on Lehigh Valley Railroad property. The hobos were happy to tell us horrid stories of the atrocities they'd suffered at the hands of the infamous Detective Campbell. And our parents were no less willing to embellish tales of his delight in heaping punishments upon wayward or miscreant kids. Detective Campbell was reputedly a law unto himself; the established judicial system had no authority on railroad property. Only Detective

Campbell did. It was a convenient way for parents to enforce, in a left-handed way, the edict: "Don't play near the railroad tracks!" For all the details we knew about Detective Campbell, not one of us had ever seen him, which made him all the more awe-inspiring.

When I left my hometown, I took some of the hobos and Detective Campbell with me. On a visit back to Jim Thorpe some years ago, a former grade school classmate (who'd stayed put) made the comment that you can't take Jim Chunk out of the native Chunker. He's right. But it's sometimes necessary to take a giant step away in order to get a better view, to see the ghosts of Railroad Detective Campbell and the great dead Indian athlete. And to hear again the faraway stories of a group of ragged men sipping strong coffee under a railroad bridge.

Dorothy "Dot" Herman would marry Andrew "Shorty" Benyo and have four children.

"Shotgun!" In my Uncle Richie's car. What? No seatbelt?

Yes, Dorothy liked to knit. And Drew and I were the lucky recipients of that hobby.

Never trust a bearded stranger, especially when he doesn't want to hear about your deep, deep desire for a Red Ryder BB gun.

Flanked by Drew and across-the-street neighbor Raymond Otto; they has just received their First Holy Communion.

Ah, the joys of motherhood! Barbara (left) was always fascinated by the fact that Kathleen never liked to have her photo taken. The drawer just over Drew's left ear is where the Old Man kept his Pall Malls.

Santa finally relented and from that day forward there was never
another Communist seen skulking about in the South Street environs.

The Subterraneans

Most young boys go through a number of phases during their formative years. At least they used to — back in the days when they were allowed to grow up at their own speed. Due to major sociological shifts, some of these phases have been either programmed out or transformed. Let me describe one of the most important of these kid phases — The Hidden Weapons Phase.

The Hidden Weapons Phase involves a fantasy that somewhere there is a great cache of incredible weapons that, once accessed, will bestow upon the young boy powers he does not normally enjoy. He is, of course, merely a *kid*; everyone around him is bigger and wields more power and authority. But all he needs to do to solve all his problems is find the secret doorway to the hidden weapons cache.

(The Hidden Weapons Phase is, in most cases, a thing of the past because, in today's world, most children don't feel powerless. In fact, in many instances, they are the ones who wield the power. They dictate to their parents what will and will not happen. This leads me to the conclusion that there may be a lot of parents walking around today still harboring the fantasy that they will find the cache of hidden weapons — that they can then use on Junior.) Today, there are video game versions of The Hidden Weapons Phase. But, of course, there were no video games in 1955. I'll tell you how it was then.

The young boy's life was daily dominated by parents, grandparents, aunts and uncles, teachers, priests, coaches, and adults in general — and for the truly desperate few, by older siblings bent on nothing short of total domination. In many cases, we were spared that last indignity because, being Baby Boomers, we were generally first-borns.

Growing up in an area where men worked underground made it logical to imagine that the weapons cache was in a cave — not unlike The Bat Cave. And we were very familiar with The Bat Cave. On hot summer days when we just wanted to get away from everything and everyone, it was common practice to stuff a pile of comic books (including, of course, *Detective Comics* and *Batman*) into a paper bag and crawl through a drainage pipe into a culvert. There we'd while away a few hours as traffic buzzed by ten feet above our heads, and the occasional, still-burning cigarette butt, tossed into the street, rained down on our baseball caps and threatened to set our comic books on fire.

Yeah, the secret cave with its cache of weapons was familiar to most of us. We knew its layout, its inventory of tanks and planes and guns and ammo, and we knew its general location. That's because Jackie McHugh told us all about it.

Jackie McHugh lived across the street and up a few houses from us. He was two years older than we were and was the leader of our little South Street Gang. Tomboy Patsy Bronko was his right-hand "man" — she was older than we were, too. Jackie McHugh remained somewhat of a mystery to us because, although he lived on the east side of town with us, he went to the Irish-Catholic Immaculate Conception School on the other side of the river, up on Broadway, near the jail.

Jackie McHugh was a born leader. He knew exactly how to play us against each other. He knew how to make promises he knew he wasn't going to keep. And he was real good at browbeating us and occasionally getting us into trouble by forcing us to do things we knew darn well we weren't supposed to do — like stealing cigarettes for him and Patsy, while we made do with dried-out mountain-laurel-leaf cigars. It was Jackie McHugh who flipped the ON button to The Hidden Weapons Phase in us.

We were all sitting in a rough circle amidst the mountain laurel bushes off the path that led from the road next to the lumberyard down in Ruddle's Run (a.k.a. The Shit Creek). We were on a ledge about twenty feet above the road, huddled in a little open spot next to an outcropping of rock. I don't remember which of us it was, but somebody was smarting from having been whupped at home — for being late to supper the night before.

Jackie puffed on an unfiltered Camel. He didn't quite have it down yet so that it looked natural and cool, but every once in a while he did manage to exhale cigarette smoke through his nostrils. I wondered, in passing, why the smoke was one color when it went into his mouth and a different color when it came out. The Surgeon General hadn't yet come up with any decisive statements regarding cigarette smoking.

"I'm gonna show you somethin' secret," Jackie said.

Being the incarnation of dumb shits that we were, we all leaned in as if he were going to distribute samples of gold coins. Instead, he shifted his weight and reached into the right-hand back pocket of his blue jeans. He pulled out a black wallet! A wallet! This was the height of sophistication. Only people who owned and regularly used folding money had need of a wallet. *We* carried our pennies (and nickels, when we were flush) and chewing gum in the front pockets of our jeans, where it could all mix collegially with the lint and stray silver foil we kept there.

His wallet was some kind of fake leather — vinyl or something. It had fake stitching around the edge, as though he'd made it at summer day camp. He dropped it onto the ground in front of his crossed legs and started his story:

"The reason Bear Mountain is important," he said, waving his cigarette-free hand up toward the mountainside — we were sitting on what would have been one of the front claws of Bear Mountain — "is because it was a holy place to the Indians. Where they buried their chiefs. Regular Indians didn't get to get buried here — just chiefs."

"And then the White Eyes came," he (who had a television set at home and who watched cowboy shows as avidly as monkeys eat bananas) continued. "They could see there was something important about the mountain, and they stayed away from it at first."

"Is that why they settled overtown?" Raymond Otto asked. His reference to *overtown* meant Mauch Chunk proper: Broadway, Susquehanna Street, the Carbon County Court House, etc. — everything across the river.

"Yeah, yeah," Jackie said. "Sure. That's right. What? Are they managing to teach you little shits something up there at St. Joe's?" he asked and smiled, then took a luxurious drag from his cigarette. Raymond nodded, completely oblivious to the sarcasm.

"Eventually the White Eyes wiped out the Indians, and those they didn't ran for the hills," Jackie continued. "Then white people began to move over here, slowly at first. But in the meantime, uranium was discovered over past The Liberties." The Liberties was the switchback road that ran from Route 903 up to The Heights. The uranium mines were cut into the side of the mountain along the highway and had been boarded up as a uranium reserve — should America ever need to build a lot more atom bombs. We sometimes removed boards from the entrances of the uranium mines and went back into them far enough that when we turned off our flashlights we experienced total, absolute darkness.

I knew from local history that Jackie had things out of chronological sequence. People had built homes in East Mauch Chunk long before uranium was discovered just west of The Liberties. But I was in languorish summer mode and didn't want to further slow down the story by correcting him. Besides which, I also didn't want to get the shit beaten out of me.

"With that valuable uranium buried in the mountain, the government knew that it would have to guard it from the Commies," he continued. "So while some house-building was taking place over here, the government snuck in and began doing some building of its own — right directly into the side of Bear Mountain. Then they hit some of the old Indian caverns and expanded them so they could store stuff there in case the army had to defend the uranium mines from the Commie bastards."

"What kind of stuff?" Junior Reis wanted to know. Ol' Jackie had lit a fire behind the eyes of just about everyone sitting in that circle and he knew it. And he knew just how to stoke it for maximum effect.

"I'll get to that," he said, flicking his exhausted cigarette butt into the mountain laurels. He pointed at one of the two Franko kids, who immediately crawled into the dried, dead leaves under the mountain laurel bush to make sure the butt was dead and wouldn't flare up and start a fire.

Raymond Otto was rocking back and forth in anticipation. I was mentally running through various "stuffs" that could have been stored inside the caverns by the federal government. But I was also wondering how they'd managed to keep it quiet while they were digging mines and caverns right in the midst of hundreds of people. So I asked. "Ha-ha-how da-da-did they keep it . . . the da-da-digging, sa-sa-secret?"

"They dug at night, with special secret lights that nobody could see, dammit."

I molded my lips into the shape of an "Oh."

The Franko kid crawled out of the mountain laurel bush fashioning a cigar from dried laurel leaves. He unselfconsciously pulled a battered matchbook from his pocket and fired it up. The dried leaves caught immediately, giving off the aroma of a forest fire.

"You'll stunt your growth, runt!" Patsy Bronko said.

"So come on, come on," Junior Reis said. "What'd they store in the mountain?"

Jackie looked around slowly, as though reading in each of our minds exactly what we'd want them to store inside our mountain. "Lotsa stuff. Tanks. Special tanks. Tanks that almost nobody in the world knows about. With special secret treads and super-quiet motors — and with wings that they can push out so they can fly."

Tanks were one of my weaknesses — tanks and rocket ships. When my father left the army, he smuggled out a bunch of stuff, including training manuals. Drew and I found them piled in the crawl space in the attic where Dorothy and Shorty stored seasonal stuff, like the Christmas tree decorations. (They also had a box of books there, including an art book with a color picture of *The Naked Maja*, which would play a large role in my sexual growth, but that's another story.)

Among the army manuals, my favorite was one that included illustrations of how to camouflage an army tank under trees and cover it with bushes to make it invisible to enemy fighter planes. Oh yes, tanks were my thing. Jackie McHugh had pulled my string.

Like a puppeteer twitching more strings, Jackie went down the list of hidden treasures inside the mountain, and, one by one, the heads of the gang nodded, or smiles erupted. Junior Reis liked the sound of "*bazookas*" and Raymond Otto found a soft spot for "*hand grenades.*" Catfish thought "*rockets and missiles*" sounded mighty fine. (I refrained, so as not to spoil the moment, from asking Jackie if he knew the difference between the two.)

The litany of goodies stashed in The Secret Cave ran from experimental planes and Tommy guns to half-track armored vehicles and flying suits. It was a deep dive into military pornography. The testosterone flowed like lava from a volcano.

None of us knew the psychology behind our reactions. We didn't know that we saw the fantasy of each new military wonder that Jackie dragged out as power — what today we would call *empowerment* — against the authoritarian suppression we felt from the adults in our lives. We would finally be able to wield some power ourselves. We wouldn't be pushed around like little kids anymore.

This newly promised power also extended to control over the older kids in the neighborhood (or in school) who dumped on us, shoved us around and belittled us, and, in general, made our lives miserable. Man oh man! We were on a roll now, getting pumped up and heated and ready at any moment to take action and revolt. It apparently never occurred to Jackie and Patsy that once we got our hands on the control levers of a flying tank, we might rebel against their co-dictatorship of our little gang. Of course, that hadn't yet occurred to us, either — at least not at the conscious level.

When he was finished with his description of The Secret Cave and its treasures, Jackie paused for dramatic effect — and to let the hook set itself in each of us. We wallowed in our macho fantasies like pigs in poop. There, amidst the mountain laurel bushes, deaf to the shouts of the men working in the lumberyard across the road, the real world effectively veiled from us, we were deeply and inexorably hooked.

Jackie slowly and carefully reached for the wallet he'd set in front of us like a talisman. He picked it up gently, as though it were a land mine. He turned it over in his hands as if he'd just found it. Someone inside the lumberyard yelled to someone else about needing two-by-eights. Jackie turned the wallet over and over, drawing out the torturous suspense.

"To get into the cave you need to have the secret identification," he said. "The door is made out of foot-thick steel. You couldn't blast it open with an atom bomb."

He opened the wallet so only he could see what was inside. Then he gazed at it as though it held the secrets of nuclear fission and a cure for cancer. Several of the guys had literally begun to quiver in anticipation. (I was being cool about it. Curious, yes, but a cool curious. I hadn't sucked down any mountain laurel smoke, so I wasn't especially zinged on Pennsylvania nicotine.)

With the speed and efficiency of a rattlesnake strike, Jackie turned the wallet toward us so we could see the secret I.D. In a balletic countermove, the gang of us leaned forward like a clutch of baby rattlesnakes ready for our mom to teach us how to strike like lightning.

Drew was the first to respond. He'd been unusually quiet up to this point, in one of his gray moods — not quite dark and menacing, but gray and neutral — not really caught up in the excitement with the rest of us. His response was classic Drew: "Huh?" Always the skeptic, he followed up with a "*Come on!*"

"'Huh' is right," Junior Reis confirmed. There was some snickering around the circle — not a good sign for a reigning dictator. Revolt, a dictator can deal with that; derision, no way.

What we were all gazing upon, the supreme secret identification to get into the extremely secret mountain cave, was a logo from Dell Comics that had been cut from the upper-left-hand corner of the front cover of a comic book! It was displayed in all its glory behind a piece of clear plastic — where most guys would have had a picture of their best girl. In Jackie McHugh's case, even though they were not a hot item, that would have been Patsy Bronko — who, at the moment, was working up a threatening look meant to still our restiveness. There was also a frown line between her eyebrows, which I read as confusion, indicating that, like us, she had been in the dark on this whole Dell Comics I.D. deal—and perhaps on The Secret Cave as well.

The absurdity of a Dell Comics logo as a secret identification was having its most profound effect on those of us who were true comic book aficionados—which in those days included most kids. We traded comic books as avidly as we traded baseball cards. Every male comic book commando knew that DC Comics—not Dell—was the king, the top of the pyramid, *El Supremo*. (The Marvel Comics of *The Fantastic Four* had not yet hit the racks and many of the great comic heroes of the 1940s, like *Captain America* and *Captain Marvel*, had died out.) DC published *Superman*, and *Batman*, and *Wonder Woman*, and *Aquaman*, and on, and on, and on. Dell Comics published . . . what? We had to rack our brains to remember anything worth a dime that Dell published. What? Dell published *Beetle Bailey*, and *Bozo*, and *Bugs Bunny*, and *Daffy Duck*, and *Dale Evans, Queen of the West*, for God's sake!

What kind of a self-respecting action hero—like those gathered around the woodland circle—would go to the foot-thick steel door of The Secret Cave, to check out a flying tank or a bazooka to save the neighborhood, by showing a dumb Dell Comics logo? We couldn't imagine.

Off to my right, Drew repeated his first response: "Huh?" In a single word he had summed up our frustration.

Seeing his sway over us beginning to evaporate before his eyes, Jackie McHugh muttered to himself and began to make conciliatory sounds, while, to his left, Patsy Bronko began to inch her right hand to the right-rear pocket of her jeans. I knew what that meant. That's where she kept her pocketknife—the biggest, longest, meanest knife in the gang. She was getting ready to defend herself if things got ugly.

But now Jackie was holding up his hand to still the disturbance. It was barely working. "Look. Look," he said. "Don't you guys get it?" His gaze swept over us from side to side, sizing us up, knowing he couldn't run from us if things went downhill. He was big and bulky, while we were lean and mean. "You gotta use Dell because . . . because . . . well, because nobody'd expect it."

The gang stilled.

Pretty slick. He had us there. Nobody, but nobody, would expect the secret sign to be a dumb Dell Comics logo. It was Jackie McHugh's version of Edgar Allan Poe's case of "The Purloined Letter." It was so obvious as to be completely missed. (Not that Jackie McHugh had ever heard of Edgar Allan Poe *or* the purloined letter.)

"Lemme see it," Junior Reis said, reaching toward Jackie's genuine high-end vinyl wallet. Jackie pulled it back reflexively. I wasn't sure if he was protecting his folding money from the rabble or didn't want any sticky kid's hands groping his precious wallet.

"Here," he said. "I'll hold it up so you can see it." And he did. We all leaned forward and gazed upon the talisman, the secret key to warfare nirvana, the sign of martial violence — violence only in self-defense, of course.

The Dell logo had been cut off the cover of a comic book (Please don't let it have been *Daffy Duck*!) in a rather ragged fashion. But then, that was Jackie McHugh's style: ragged, undisciplined, bordering on careless. And, with a mob of first-borns in the crowd (Catfish, Raymond Otto, Junior, one of the Franko kids, myself), the fact that the logo wasn't exactly centered in the clear plastic window and was, in fact, a little crooked, caused us to regard it less as we would a Catholic holy card leading us to the True Faith, and more as just a cheap way to get into armory heaven.

"Sa-sa-so okay," I spat out. "Wha-wha-wha-where's the door?"

"Yeah," came several responses from the Peanut Gallery. "The door."

I had a clear, face-to-face view of Jackie's expression because I was sitting directly across from him. The shadow that passed over his face didn't boost my spirits a whole helluva lot. The shadow threatened to become a storm cloud as Patsy Bronko dug her elbow into his ribs and demanded to know: "Yeah. Where's the door?"

This may have been the first time Jackie McHugh had gone it alone, cooking up a cockeyed plot all on his own without running it past Patsy or one of his friends in one of the higher grades at school. His eyebrows went up slightly and I swear you could actually see the 20-watt light bulb go on over his head.

"Well, you see, that's just it."

"What?" Drew demanded to know, sniffing the blood in the water. Drew hadn't said much, had barely taken part in this whole session, except at the critical times. His instincts had cut in, and he was becoming increasingly suspicious and skeptical.

"It's just that, you know, it's one of the rules (the main rule, in fact, at least after having the secret I.D.) that everybody's gotta earn the right to enter the secret steel door by being smart enough and resourceful enough" — he pulled the word *resourceful* out with an obvious strain; where he'd picked it up, I had no idea — "to find the door in the first place." A sigh — subtle, to be sure — escaped his lips. He'd gotten his sorry ass off the hot grill two times in ten minutes. He was on a roll.

"You mean we gotta find a door," said one of the Franko kids — whether Dave or Mike, I don't know — "somewhere in this big mountain?" His gaze rolled up to the immensity of the mountain rising to the sky behind Jackie McHugh.

"Yeah, yeah," Jackie said. "Yeah."

And so began a week of explorations that would have made Admiral Byrd proud.

We put together a schedule in which we paired up gang members with each other to explore precisely defined segments of Bear Mountain. We started our controlled roving immediately after eating our Wheaties in the morning and continued, with a break for lunch, until our mothers came to the bank above The Dump to call us home for supper. Not everyone could make it every day. Some family vacations and other commitments intruded, but typically, most days, there were a half-dozen goofy kids scrambling over the mountain like a little army of ants on top of a melting lollipop.

We weren't running blind. We knew exactly what we were looking for because, during the heat of the search, we had plenty of time to compare notes about what each of us thought the foot-thick steel door looked like, and how it was probably tucked beneath an overhang of rock, which made it impossible to spot from the air. We also surmised that the door was not stainless steel or any type of steel that was reflective, because if it were, the rising or setting sun would have shone off it, revealing its location to anyone who bothered to look up at the mountain, morning or evening.

During that week, we found a lot of stuff that had been abandoned on the mountainside — everything from a dead dog to parts of a car that looked as though it was built in the 1920s. How the car pieces — and they were big pieces — managed to get halfway up the side of a mountain that had no roads stumped us.

During the week, Jackie McHugh made himself fairly scarce. He wasn't about to give us any hints about where The Secret Cave was located, and he wasn't about to put himself into a place where our frustration at the end of a long, hot day might be taken out on him. Ditto with Patsy Bronko, who we were certain hadn't been in the loop beforehand, and who was obviously none too happy about her devalued status in the hierarchy of the gang.

By Saturday afternoon we had just about had it when two pair of us bumped into each other about fifty yards above Pleasant Hill. We had been making sweeps of our designated sectors and we came together at the edge that joined the two zones. It was a lesson in why dictators have rules against citizens getting together in groups. Too much information is exchanged — sandwiched between sessions of bitching about the poor performance of the boss. Emotions begin to heat as grievances are aired and plots to overthrow the ruling elite are hatched.

Catfish was getting just plain tired of all this trudging around the side of the mountain; it was too much like work. Maurice Otto — a born labor union member who anchored the end of the bell curve where the malcontents live — agreed with Fish. Junior Reis was just plain frustrated by the whole damned thing. We were putting in a whole lot of work and getting nothing out of it, and Jackie McHugh didn't show us anything in writing that indicated that he couldn't give us a hint where the door was. Besides, he was getting too big for his britches anyway, always bossing us around as though we were little kids or something. For my part, I agreed with all the moiling discontent and frustration.

Because we'd been assigned sectors for the day, we knew where Drew and Raymond Otto and the two Franko kids were, so we went off to plot a coup — or to come up with an alternate way of getting into The Secret Cave. Unfortunately, we chose the latter. And what a bone-headed decision that turned out to be.

We concluded that we didn't want to take over the gang — doing that would be too much like leadership, work which none of us was very experienced at. We would merely do the political thing: we would slow down the doings of the gang for the summer by not showing up. Jackie and Patsy could be king and queen of . . . nothing.

The eight of us wandered down off the side of the mountain and returned to the laurel-shrouded rock ledge where all of this craziness had begun. We sat in a circle and hashed it out. It took all of ten minutes.

At the time, it seemed like a brilliant solution to our predicament. We would dig into the side of the mountain until we came up against a wall of The Secret Cave, whereupon we would punch our way through to the inside. Our thinking went like this: Considering all of the military equipment and supplies The Secret Cave contained (and that was considerable), the cave itself must be pretty darned big. So, it would be a lot easier to find the cave than it would be to find the steel door that allowed entry — a door that might very well be camouflaged behind a wall of greenery, which means we'd never find it by conventional means.

So we would commence tunneling a horizontal mineshaft into the side of the mountain until we hit the bonanza!

And where would we begin this mining endeavor?

Right there.

That decision had a sort of beauty to it. The whole affair had begun there, and the thing would end there when we dug into the mountain and encountered our heart's desire — the means to destroy anything or anyone that stood in our way.

We eyed the little green clearing among the mountain laurel where we sat. We eyed the slate outcropping that gave the place its personality. And then our collective IQ dropped roughly fifty points. "We can start in on that rock," Catfish said, pointing at one of the fifteen-foot-tall slate outcroppings. "We'll crack it up and haul it away and it will leave a big hole that we can expand."

We jumped up and surveyed the rock where our efforts would begin. We ran our dirty hands over its smooth surface, so smooth that it seemed to be chiseled by Michelangelo, possibly as a base for one of his statues. The slate was stacked like the dorsal fin of a shark coming out of the Earth. The hunks of slate were cracked, but cracked in a divinely parallel way, as though cut by masons. The slab we'd picked as our starting place was the biggest single piece in the outcropping. It stood fifteen feet tall from the surface of the forest to its tip. How far down into the Earth it went, we had no idea — at least not yet.

For eight weary, snot-nosed, grimy-fingernailed guys, we were plenty excited. "It's too late to start today and tomorrow's Sunday and we gotta go to church," Junior Reis said. "Let's start first thing Monday. Everybody bring tools." We all agreed. We further agreed that if we ran into Jackie or Patsy, we'd come up with some excuse as to why we couldn't get together with them and the rest of the gang. Hell, we had the best excuse possible: We're still looking for that idiotic door. So, Monday it would be — the start of our workweek.

When Monday morning came, it found a gang of potential miners and engineers gathered at the clearing. The eight of us stood before the slate outcropping the way the space-suited moon explorers stood before the onyx monolith on the moon in *2001: A Space Odyssey*. Scattered around the clearing were our tools — a pathetic assortment of throwaway hammers and rope and junk our fathers had discarded as broken or useless. In among the hardware, there were three railroad spikes that would turn out to be the most practical tools in the whole stash.

Hoping to reignite the enthusiasm of Saturday afternoon, breaking us out of just standing around the slate monolith in awe, Catfish grabbed a claw hammer and swung it at the hunk of slate. The blow, administered by the biggest guy among us, chipped off a piece of rock the size of a dime. I don't know if it was real or if he was pretending, but Fish groaned as though the blow had sent an electric pain up his arm. "Let's go," he said. "We got work to do."

We all grabbed something and started vying with each other to get close enough to get in a blow. It was immediately obvious we were not all going to be able to work on the face of the rock at the same time. We broke up into two teams of four, taking turns at taking on the rock face. We made a lot of banging and cracking noise to augment the noises coming up from the nearby lumberyard.

We never stopped to think whether the guys who worked across the little road in the lumberyard would call the cops on us for disturbing the peace and destroying private property. If they did, what kind of a lame excuse would we give them? That we were burrowing into the side of the mountain in hopes of encountering (Ssshhhhhh!) The Secret Cave? They'd haul us off to the bughouse. We ignored the possibility and just plain forged ahead, as though we had no other purpose for being on Earth than burrowing down into it.

By our lunch break, it was apparent that we were not inflicting much damage on the slab of slate. There were chips here and there, but no cracks. Junior Reis, always a worrier, wondered out loud just how far down into the ground the damned slate outcropping went. "What if it goes down another twenty or thirty feet?"

"Then we dig down twenty or thirty feet and get it out," Catfish said.

"What's the point?" Drew asked, in a blaze of logic. "We're supposed to be going *into* the mountain on this level, not digging down toward the center of the Earth."

That caused Catfish to pause and reconsider the direction of his digging. "Then I guess we'll have to break it off at ground level."

"Couldn't we blow it up?" Raymond Otto asked.

"You have any dynamite sitting around?" his brother Maurice wanted to know.

"No," Raymond admitted. "But we could get some."

"You go get some," Catfish said. "We'll wait here for you."

Raymond shrugged his shoulders, pulled himself up off the ground, hitched up his pants, walked over to the slab of slate and took another whack at it. He grimaced as shock waves fed themselves back through the handle of the hammer.

I walked over and came up with the only good suggestion I'd generated in the last week. "Why don't we ya-ya-use the railroad sa-sa-spikes and wa-wa-wedge them ba-ba-between two of the sa-sa-slabs to sa-sa-separate 'em?" Why, indeed?

A brilliant idea, by its very light, can stir even the most dedicated slacker. In a moment, the rock face was swarming with kids moving away little clumps of dirt, looking for places where we could insert the railroad spikes. We began hammering one in as high as we could go, somehow intuiting the concept of the fulcrum, figuring the crack was the most susceptible the farthest from its base.

It was.

In less than an hour we hammered the spike five inches into the crack — which separated the foremost two slabs by about an inch. That inch decreased the farther down the rock face the crack went, but the little expansion of the crack was enough to open the rock for the insertion of the next spike. We placed it about eighteen inches lower and began hammering. In less than an hour the top spike fell out because the second spike had opened the gap more than one-and-a-half inches at the top.

We reinserted the first spike, but this time another eighteen inches below the second spike, and once again we enlarged the separation between the two slabs of slate. Junior inserted a spare hammerhead (minus a handle) into the now three-inch-wide gap at the top so it wouldn't close on us, and we hammered more spikes in, lower and lower.

Even goofy nine-year-olds grasp a concept occasionally, and, one by one, we were getting the idea that by separating the front slab from its supporting brother, we had weakened it. When we began whacking it now, it would not have the combined strength of the entire outcropping to resist us. The separated slab *didn't* resist us much longer. It lasted only two days.

Like the apes that figure out that a sappy twig shoved down an anthill captures ants on its sticky surface, the twig thus qualifying as a "tool," our band of miners became creative with their accumulation of "tools." Junior found a rebar with a hunk of really hard concrete on the end of it that served as a sledgehammer. Catfish found a ten-inch-diameter hunk of steel — that came off a '52 Olds his father was working on at his service station — and, with a rope passed through the hole in the center, it became a mace that could be swung against the resisting slab of slate. We were like a more positive version of the pack of boys in *Lord of the Flies*; we were working together as we *never* had under the dictatorship of Jackie McHugh and Patsy Bronko.

But it was too good to last. Less than a week into the mining operation, the news of our enterprise leaked, and Jackie McHugh, along with Patsy Bronko and transient gang member Matt King, showed up at our worksite. We weren't really surprised when they arrived. I think we'd been aware that eventually they were going to find out what we were doing because our absence from the South Street scene was so profound.

"What're you kids doin' here?" demanded Jackie, flanked by his two flunkies.

"What the [expletive deleted] does it look like we're doing?" Drew said. "We're lookin' for The [expletive deleted] Secret Cave."

What was Jackie McHugh supposed to say to that? *He* was the one who put us on to what several of us were beginning to suspect was a wild goose chase. *He* was the one too stubborn to tell us where the entrance was — because there was no entrance. He was trapped like a mackerel in a cook pot.

He couldn't very well dissuade us from our mining enterprise unless he either told us where the steel door was or admitted that he'd made the whole damned thing up. All he could do was stand there looking unhappy that we were doing something without his supervision. He obviously hadn't told Patsy Bronko about The Secret Cave in the first place, much less let her in on the fact that it was all made up. (And Matt King? Nobody liked Matt King. He was a wise-ass and a punk. Eddie Haskell to our Beaver Cleaver. But an Eddie Haskell who enjoyed following through on being just plain nasty.)

"We got work to do," Junior said, and went back to work taking whacks at the now vulnerable slab that had been separated from its support system. It wasn't like Jackie, Patsy, and Matt King were going to pitch in and help us. And after a few smokes, the tiresome trio walked off. "Stupid babies," Matt King muttered.

As before, we took turns working on the slab in four-kid teams — a half-hour on, a half-hour lounging around reading comic books and smoking dried-out laurel leaves. Our work was making quite a racket, but there was no retaliation from the workers in the lumberyard. They just went on with their work and their cursing at the planks they had to stack or load on trucks.

Before lunch on the second day, the slab had been separated from its fellows; a crack began to appear one-third of the way down its face. That spurred us on to greater efforts. The crack spread, and within ten minutes we knew we had it. Better still, the crack wasn't perfectly horizontal, but went along the surface at an angle, so that one of Drew's blows was just enough to dislodge the thing and with a crack and a slip, it fell to the ground, making a *thump* like a box of geography books being dropped on a classroom floor. Fortunately, it happened slowly enough that everyone involved was able to jump out of the way in time.

We let out a collective "Whoop!" and careened about like a bunch of drunken monkeys.

Now what?

We pried an edge of it up off the ground and stood it on end. It looked like a square wheel, the kind you'd see in a cartoon about the caveman who invented the first wheel and didn't know what it was.

"Let's get it out of here," I said. "Pa-pa-push it over the sa-sa-side."

We did. We rolled it to the edge of the trail and let it drop down into the ditch that ran along beside the dirt road. It made enough noise that we were sure we were going to be the object of the lumberyard workers' attention. We set the springs in our legs to take off, like a bunch of roused ruffled grouse, into the woods behind us. But nothing happened. Nobody from the lumberyard stirred in our direction.

We decided to celebrate by having lunch early. We walked another fifty yards along the trail to the big open spot with the ledge that hung out over the drainage ditch — beside which the lumberyard piled sand that they sold to construction crews. We were successful miners, effectively plying our trade. We lounged around on the grass, ate our peanut butter and jam sandwiches, and talked tough.

From that day on, we used the bigger, wider spot of ground for our strategy meetings and for our lunch breaks. We overlooked the lumberyard office, which sat across the parking lot, straddling The Shit Creek. Thirty feet below the ledge that stuck out over the ditch there was a pile of white sand. It had been dumped there because there wasn't enough space for it in the concrete bin where they stored the sand and gravel. Beyond the sand was the single line of railroad track they used to bring in boxcars filled with lumber.

A few weeks later, this ledge and this sand would be the scene of one of my childhood triumphs. It happened like this:

After the first hunk of slate was broken off, we worked like maniacs to crack off more of it, which we did on a fairly regular basis. We were dropping an average of two more slabs down into the ditch per week.

Apparently bored without their army of knuckleheads, Jackie McHugh, Patsy Bronko, and Matt King made periodic visits to our mine. One such visit came during our lunch break over on the flat spot above the ledge. As we sometimes did — as our stomachs absorbed the nutritional goodness of gobs of peanut butter — we talked about how somebody ought to try jumping off the ledge into the little pile of white sand. The jump would have to be technically correct in that the jumper would need to get a running start and leap out from the ledge in order to clear the ditch and make it into the softer sand.

Most of us in the gang were fairly good at running and jumping and the things testosterone-fueled boys are good at. Raymond Otto wasn't all that good, due in large part to his mother spending every waking hour on a campaign to scare him about just about everything on Earth. His younger brother Maurice — we called him The Whistler because he whistled ceaselessly — paid no heed to their mother and was liable to do anything the rest of us did. The

Franko kids, a year apart but looking like a big and little edition of the same kid, were good at the boy stuff. Same with Junior Reis; he was always ready, like a cocked spring. Catfish, the biggest of us all, was a bit more cowardly than one would expect from someone of his bulk. Drew and I were not beyond running up to Big Rock on the top of Bear Mountain and down the other side, and then running around the base of the mountain along the railroad tracks just for the hell of it.

One day, the visiting Matt King got it into his pus-filled head to get on our case about making the jump. "Ah, shit. Yer all a bunch of babies. Ain't none of you ever gonna do it. Shit," he said, taking a long puff of a purloined Chesterfield. He came back — three lunch breaks in a row — and started in on the same theme each time. He was fingernails-on-a-blackboard annoying.

"You're so hopped about it, you go do it," one of the Franko kids said.

"Yer a bunch of chickenshits," Matt King said.

"Ain't," the ever loquacious Catfish said.

"Are so," Matt King said.

And on, and on, and on.

By the third spoiled lunch break, I'd had it. "Ah-ah-ah-I'll da — da-do it," I volunteered. "Ba-ba-ba-but then ya-ya-ya-you gotta do it," meaning Big Mouth Matt King. "Da-deal?"

"Yeah. Yeah, sure," he said. "Chickenshit."

"Ya-ya-ya-you all ha-ha-heard him," I said.

"Yep," came the universal response.

Now, I wasn't an especially impulsive kid. First-borns usually aren't. But I'd thought about this. I wasn't especially brave or especially foolhardy. But neither was I afraid of my shadow. I'd climbed to the tiptop of trees where nobody else would climb, and hadn't yet broken my neck. *Besides*, I asked myself, *how much can it hurt?*

Without further ado, without fanfare or dramatic buildup, I got up, walked back as far as I could go into the little clearing so I could make use of as much runway as possible, and I started to jog toward the ledge. Everyone got sucked to their feet at the same time and jogged along with me toward the edge.

In the backyard of our house, I could easily clear three-foot-tall hedges, so I had no doubt about propelling myself out far enough that I'd land in the sand. Unless, of course, I tripped before I launched. But I didn't. I hit the tip of the ledge and launched myself into space. And for a long, glorious, exhilarating moment, I was airborne. It seemed to go on forever. And ever. Like sailing through space in zero gravity.

But, of course, gravity *was* in play — very much so. The ground was suddenly coming up at me very quickly, the white sand pile growing larger. I relaxed my legs at the knees, and impacted. I'd expected a jolt. There was one, but it was slight. No worse than jumping off a diving board into a pool.

I wasn't conscious of it at first, as I was still in my little spacey world, but the gang was cheering and shouting as they stood along the edge of the clearing thirty feet above. Someone from the lumberyard office came to the door and yelled, "What the hell're you kids doin' up there?" Then he went back inside.

There was a series of outcroppings ten yards away from the ledge which you could crawl up to reach the clearing above. A little spring ran out of the side of the outcropping. I ran over to the rocks and clambered up, and before anyone could even pat me on the back, I jogged back across the clearing and threw myself out into the air. Again, the feeling of ultimate liberation — of floating, flying, soaring. And again the little jolt at landing.

"Wow!" one of the guys said. "He likes it."

I crawled back up the rocks and the gang hauled me into the clearing. Matt King was conspicuously not among them. He stood way off to the side. I broke loose from the rough congratulations from my friends and walked over to Matt King. Slowly and elaborately, like a fancy maitre d' directing a diner to his table, I extended my arm toward the ledge. "Well?" I said.

For a moment Matt King was without words. Finally, he said, "Fuck you!" threw down his half-smoked Chesterfield, and walked off. He never came back to what, by this time, we were calling The Mine. And his influence within the gang was never again a factor.

We continued to work on The Mine all summer long, but with diminishing enthusiasm. We spent more time socializing, lying about, smoking dried mountain laurel leaves, and shooting the shit. At the rate we were removing the slate and dropping it down to the ditch below, it would take us a million years to tunnel into the mountain. The hole we'd spent the summer digging was just about big enough to hold a medium-sized houseplant.

And anyway, by that time we knew that there was no Secret Cave. We had come to know it as our hard work got us so little in return. Of course, our mothers loved The Mine because it kept us occupied and out of their hair, and they always knew where they could find us. It had become the new Dusty Trail.

With the end of summer came the beginning of another school year, and we weren't all going to the same school. We would occasionally get together at The Mine on an autumn Saturday to peck at the unyielding slate, but we were dropping fewer and fewer rocks over the side of the ledge.

Occasionally I'd jump off the ledge in the bigger, higher clearing, but eventually someone bought the sand, and I wasn't inclined to leap up and out only to land on hard ground.

We saw little if anything of Jackie McHugh and Patsy Bronko, even though they still lived on the same block. Once in a while, we'd see one of them from afar, but we didn't hail them. They went to a different school and they moved in different circles — and perhaps, I thought, they sat at the bottom of the totem pole in that alternate social structure.

I moved to California in 1977, and on the occasional trip home to Jim Thorpe, I'd go out and lope along the old dirt road that ran under the ledge that supported The Mine. The slabs of slate we had so laboriously scratched from the hillside were still there in a rough pile in the ditch. A little farther down the road was the ledge I'd jumped from.

But they're all gone now — that pleasant little hillside overrun with mountain laurel and secret doors and ragged mining tools. There is no Mine, no ledge from which a wild kid could take a flying leap. In a willful frenzy, a selfish businessman took heavy equipment to the foot of Bear Mountain and raped it, tearing it apart in a sweep of environmental violence so brutal that nothing will grow there for another few decades — and even then it could only be the lowly white birch. (He planned to put in a mobile home park.)

The foot of the mountain is a mess today — a sty on the landscape. And our ledge and The Mine are gone. But they will linger in our memories — until, one by one, the eight of us blink out.

Two already have.

The Best Day Ever — Almost

In even the most miserable life, relatively speaking, there has to be one day that stands out as the best (or at least as the least miserable). That day has a texture and quality to it that makes it almost preternatural: there is a sense that the day has no boundaries, that the clock has slowed significantly or simply stopped, and that you and everyone around you is immortal. (Of course, any Halloween apple *might* hide a razor blade.)

One particularly bliss-filled day came on a Saturday in the late autumn of my ninth year, after we had pretty much given up on The Mine. I know it was late autumn because the leaves were changing and the little gardens people had planted behind their houses had been raided of everything ripe — first by the gardeners and then by the animals. And the place we played that day had been hand-harvested of the acre or so of corn that had made it through the summer; in fact, the tops of a quarter-acre of the stalks had been lopped off and burned the previous weekend, leaving three-quarters of an acre of dried but still standing stalks, browned and yellowed, outclassed by the brilliant plumage of the trees bordering the field.

We were somewhat out of our comfort zone. We (meaning The South Street Gang) were across the dividing line, which was Third Street — the same Third and South Streets where the Coal Man lived on the corner. As a result, on that Saturday we were intermingling with several other groups of kids — sort of our own little United Nations.

There was George "Puppy" Armbruster, a year older than I was, destined in his senior year in high school to play on a state championship basketball team. Jerry Strubinger and some of the other Strubinger kids were also in attendance; Jerry was the oldest. Even our resident Arab was there — Aboo Hascin, tall and skinny and Adam's apple-y, like Ichabod Crane. We were several dozen kids with nothing better to do on that balmy Saturday than play together at war. And, lurking on the periphery, was the semi-ostracized Matt King. He was into a phase of kidhood most boys go through involving the idolatry of fire.

In those days, to have a pack of matches was to have power — power to light a cigarette, to start a campfire, or to heat the tip of a pocketknife to sterilize it before gouging out a splinter from a finger. A book of matches in the pocket, even if there were only two or three left, was uplifting for the old self-esteem. You were a direct descendant of Prometheus, fire-starter for the human race.

It would be difficult, from ground level, to set the geography for that day. But fortunately, we have a couple of very reliable cartographers in the pair of elderly crows who inhabited a nest high up in one of the trees by The Swinging Bridge, that crossed the ravine where The Shit Creek ran. (The Swinging Bridge was there so that people who lived on Pleasant Hill could walk from their homes across to the mainland.)

These two mature crows were intelligent enough to have evaded the smack of copper-colored BBs for several years. They were wily; the tree they'd chosen for their home was close enough to The Swinging Bridge that no kid would chance taking a shot at them — for fear of being caught by a pedestrian using the bridge.

The crows had raised many a flock of hatchlings in that tree, and they knew the area — and the seasons — well. They knew when the elderberries were ripe and where they grew; they knew the soft lawns where a heavy rain would force the worms above ground; they knew where the abandoned crab apple trees still produced a decent crop; and they most certainly knew where the corn was planted on those years that it was, and when it was ripe enough to raid. Oh, they knew more about the cornfield than the landowner, more than the couple who planted it, and certainly more than the dopey kids who, that day, were infiltrating it.

As Poppa Crow hopped to the edge of the nest to intuit the breeze coming in from the west, he was looking at the mainland of East Mauch Chunk; he was looking up the sets of steps that led from the west end of The Swinging Bridge — a contraption of steel cables and wooden slats that was wide enough for two pedestrians to pass each other going in opposite directions burdened with two shopping bags. The steps led west to South Street. He was looking up Third Street, but a segment of Third Street that dipped gradually and then more hazardously toward the Shit Creek ravine. The fields, where we were playing that morning, were to his right.

Adjusting his ebony wings to ask the breeze to fill in under them for lift, he hopped off the edge of the nest and rose like a black kite, steering gently over the field in front of him and to his right. This field was not the field of corn, but an empty field of tall grass turning brown — where the kids from the neighborhood sometimes got together for a sandlot game of ball, but not all that frequently. The field was bordered on the south by the steps, on the west by the backyards of several houses, on the east by the Shit Creek ravine, and on the north by a line of trees that shut it off from the next field — the field where, in the upper acre, the corn was harvested.

Poppa Crew glided through the stream of air and looked down at a contraption of major appliance boxes, sewn together with shoelaces and washing line, down in the northeast corner of the empty field. It was built early in the summer as a fort, a configuration of rooms that bore a resemblance, at least on the inside, to the International Space Station: one tight room leading to another, and to another, all coming off a central hub — in this case a vertical GE refrigerator box with a flap cut in the top for the purpose of peering outside (to assess approaching danger).

As Poppa Crow surfed the breeze above the cardboard fort, he spotted a tendril of smoke issuing from one of the slit windows. The fort was occupied by Chimney Boy — the name he had given the young human who smoked but never burned — who skulked around like a feral cat. And Chimney Boy had lately been spending a great deal of time alone, sulking.

Poppa Crow adjusted his wings and rose a bit more on the air current, enough to clear the approaching line of trees. He turned northwest, cleared the tips of the trees, and came across a scene as frantic as the Chimney Boy's was lethargic.

In this field, the lower half was grass — untended, starting to turn brown in anticipation of winter. But the upper half was as frenetic as a disturbed anthill. The acre of dead cornstalks was alive with kids, rushing this way and that, moving in waves, advancing, retreating, tossing clumps of dirt clinging to the roots of topped cornstalks — dirt hand grenades exploding in puffs of smoky dust. There were lots of kids, all sorts — small, medium, nearly big, girls mixed in with the boys — all of them huffing and puffing and sweating and yelling.

The morning's battle was in full swing. The several dozen kids had divided themselves up into two roughly equal teams. The most alpha of the males took turns picking from the massed array of kids, tending to pick more of their own gang members because they knew what they were dealing with (rather than weakening their side by picking kids whose pedigree they didn't know as well). But even with that prejudice working, the teams were mixed to roughly equal talent at mayhem.

By mutual consent, the war of the day was between the Americans and the Nazis. The battles in lower East Mauch Chunk usually revolved around a Western theme, influenced not a little by all of the cowboy shows on TV. The reenactment of World War II was, that day, inspired by the observation that when you broke off the top of a cornstalk — which wasn't difficult to do, even for the girls, because the stalks were well dried-out — you had about eight inches of stalk left with a six-inch-wide clump of dirt clinging to the roots. The resulting grenade resembled the German hand grenades of World War II — commonly referred to by the American and British troops as "potato mashers" because they resembled that kitchen utensil.

Jerry Strubinger wrenched a root from the ground and threw it toward the open field, where it exploded in a spray of dirt in a very satisfying way. The weapons — an acre or so of them — were at hand. But we needed some rules. (Even war needs rules.) Well, no problem. Various kids threw out rules and they were voted on immediately by the rabble. True democracy.

No ripping up potato masher grenades from the center of the cornfield. The center would be preserved as the battleground through which the armies would creep and circulate. Rip up only grenades from the edge of the field. That rule courtesy of Jerry Strubinger, who lived only a block away and therefore had some personal attachment to the field, even though his family did not own it.

After every battle there would be an intermission of ten minutes during which we'd count up the dead and come up with a score. That, submitted by Puppy Armbruster, was unanimously accepted. Raymond Otto had received a used wristwatch for his birthday, so he was designated as timekeeper. Not happy with the burden of responsibility, he began to cry; but after being slapped on the back repeatedly in a friendly fashion, he acquiesced.

Eileen Strubinger — a pleasant girl in my class at St. Joe's (and Jerry's younger sister) — sought a provision that grenades weren't to be thrown at an enemy's face, because it could make you go blind. Accepted.

Catfish proposed that it was OK to knock an enemy down if you got close enough, but you couldn't punch him (or her) in the face. Sounded reasonable. We weren't barbarians, after all. Just doughty American GIs and Nazi scum.

"What about when you get killed?" Drew wanted to know. We picked a section of the open field and designated the left side of it the hospital where you went if you were badly wounded, and on the right side was the cemetery, where you went to lie down if you were dead. If you were wounded in only a minor way, you kept fighting. We were no cowards.

"How do we know who's who?" one of the Franko kids wanted to know. The Franko kids had been picked for opposing sides, and although they would obviously know which was which, *we* wouldn't necessarily be able to tell one from the other. "Shirts and skins," someone suggested. We did "shirts and skins" when we played basketball. One team kept their shirts on and the other took theirs off. "Sure," someone else said, "that'd work. It's warm enough."

And it was, but then the realization began to seep into the mob that fully one-third of the players were girls. Eileen Strubinger shook her head no and we knew she was right. "I got it," Drew said, and he turned and ran off down the field, returning a few moments later with an old ratty T-shirt that someone had thrown away in the woods. He began tearing it into strips and passed them around. "Tie it to your left arm," he said. And our team did. (Drew and I had managed to get on the same team. Good for us.)

But now came the most difficult decision of the day: Which team would be the heroic Americans and which would be the hated German Nazis? One confusing factor was that both sides had their share of German-Americans in the ranks. We always had trouble when it came to choosing cowboy-versus-Indian conflicts, unless the battles were scheduled the day after an episode of *Broken Arrow* on TV — in which case we all wanted to be Michael Ansara (as the Indian hero, Cochise).

But since there were no adults involved to screw up the whole thing, we settled it the only fair way: Jerry Strubinger took a nickel from his pocket and we flipped for it. So OK then, our side became the rotten Nazis, the scourge of the Earth, evil incarnate. (But, of course, if we had actually *been* them, we'd have worn nicer uniforms than the spunky American GIs.)

We now marched our respective armies to opposite sides of the cornfield and tried, as best we could, to line them up in straight rows. Most of us were from Catholic schools, so we were experts at lining up for just about everything — even for going to the bathroom. (The boys were sent into the boys' room in sets of six; the nun stood outside the open door clicking her clicker as a countdown to when we were supposed to zip up and come out so the next group could go in. Of course, every once in a while, there was a painful howl as one of the boys zipped up his fly too fast and got his little nipper caught in the zipper.) Being Catholics and Nazis meant that our side was major-league superior at lining up. We were ready.

Two of the neighborhood dogs, excited by the scent of tension, ran around in circles, barking like crazy.

I looked around. The day was warm even though the late autumn sun was lower on the horizon. The trees that surrounded the field were bright with color. A hawk or a crow circled overhead as if it were a reconnaissance plane, ready to direct various aspects of the coming battle. My fellow Jerries were lined up in an excellent fashion. I could hear individual intakes of breath, and could actually feel their effort to stay calm for the coming fray.

Even though I was still a little kid, I read as though I had a paper-and-ink-devouring tapeworm inside of me. I had already read *The Red Badge of Courage*, and I knew that not everything was going to go perfectly according to plan. Straight lines or not, real life tends to be messy — and war, even messier.

Jerry Strubinger sent one of his men around the edge of the cornfield. He held up two fingers: two minutes until the battle would commence.

Three of our older members went into a huddle and came up with our plan. We would send our oldest guys around both sides of the cornfield and when they reached the halfway-around, they'd begin going in toward the center; our younger soldiers would go directly into the maze of cornstalks, which would (hopefully) push the enemy soldiers out toward the edges, where they would run into our most elite forces.

"Is everybody armed?" someone asked.

Indeed we were. Every one of us had two potato-masher grenades. We were ready. One of the dogs, a brown and white one, came running around the edge of the cornfield, yelping, responding to the increasing tension. When he saw us, he stopped, looked behind him in the direction of the army he'd just left, and turned around and ran back — probably confused as to which mass of soldiers was more wired and threatening.

The enemy kid ran to the side of the cornfield again and held up one finger: one minute to go.

Our breathing rate increased. Kids looked at each other in mature ways, as though knowing they were about to embark on a grown-up ritual. One seven-year-old girl who I didn't recognize laughed nervously. The kid next to her gave her a little punch in the upper arm to calm her. She looked at him and nodded. She held two dirt-ball stalks, each as big as her head.

"Everybody ready!" someone at the back of the army said. We didn't look around to see who it was.

The kid ran around the side of the field again, looked back at the way he had come, nodded, and dropped his arm.

"Now!" someone yelled. We let out a collective roar and sprinted toward the corn.

As planned, our team split into three parties, the younger kids going directly into the middle, where their diminutive size would allow them to more easily maneuver through the stalks. The rest of us went around the sides of the field. I went with the side going around to the right, and we hadn't reached halfway around when we encountered three enemy soldiers coming toward us. When they saw us, they turned tail and tried to run. As though we were one organism, we — trained on a long summer of playing baseball and knocking down tin cans with rocks — lobbed our grenades after the retreating soldiers. The dirt grenades arched gracefully through the air, bits of dirt spiraling off them as they rose.

They came down in a mass, and two of the retreating kids were hit, the clumps of dirt exploding against their backs in a most satisfying way. "Dead, dead," we called. "To the cemetery." The two corpses drooped their shoulders and walked back to the cemetery as we turned and pushed our way into the forest of stalks.

We immediately lost sight of half of our men as they meshed with the stalks. Most of us were skinny as skeletons, and we were able to jitterbug our way around the tall stalks. Brushing against them, though, dusted us with decaying debris. We didn't much care.

One of the younger Strubinger boys was directly to my right, and one of the Franko kids was to my left. We peered ahead as best we could, trying to see around the wall of stalks, as though we had x-ray vision. And there was a movement ahead, far ahead. I pointed in that direction and signaled for the others to drop to their knees and stay still, which they did. We waited patiently, sweat running down our faces and chests, still breathing hard.

Sure enough, there were two of the enemy coming toward us. Something about that was wrong, though. They should not have been able to get so far so fast. Jerry Strubinger must have sent some of his soldiers into the battlefield before the signal to start was given. (Sneaky bastard! That's the kind of crap *we Nazis* were supposed to specialize in.) The two of them were coming quickly, apparently sure that we had no idea they were there.

We could hear the shouts and whistles and hoots of the battling soldiers around the edges of the field and some dimmer shouts coming from the other side of the field. The battle was joined on three fronts. It was in full fury. The two lousy cheating bastards were only thirty yards away and didn't have a clue we were there. We waited... and waited. They were coming on fast, each armed with two dirt grenades, sure that they had the jump on our side.

We waited until they were ten yards away, stood up and slaughtered them, dirt flying everywhere, the grenades bouncing off their chests. "Dead, dead," we shouted, pointing behind us as we relieved them of their unused grenades. They followed our thumbs back to the cemetery as we continued on.

One of the kids — a kid whose name I didn't know, but only knew that he lived a few blocks away on Fourth Street — muttered, "Pricks!" as he slouched off.

"Loser!" the Franko kid spat back.

We moved ahead, sidestepping the stalks, moving steadily but not too fast. We were near the center of the field. I took a moment to look up. The blue sky was nearly totally hidden by the towering stalks, their tassels yellow and golden and beginning to turn brown around the edges. A bird sailed high overhead, circling. I pretended I was in some exotic land, in the middle of battle, my blood rushing and boiling with anticipation.

The younger Strubinger boy touched my arm and pointed ahead. He'd caught sight of a movement through the stalks. We squinted and could make out someone in a blue-and-white-striped polo shirt moving across in front of us. We began to move toward him, staying a bit behind; the kid was moving cautiously, looking carefully ahead — he never thought to look behind. I signaled that we should lob the grenades into the air, above the stalks, so they'd drop onto him. We stood shoulder to shoulder and let the grenades fly. The kid never knew what hit him. One grenade hit him on the right shoulder, another on the back, and the third exploded against his left foot. "Dead!" we yelled together.

But at the same moment, a half-dozen grenades fell on us from the right side. *We* were dead — but alive enough to feel the discomfort that comes when a clump of dirt the size of a softball meets skin drenched in sweat.

"Eeeeeeggggggg!" I said.

"Uuuuuuggggghhhhh!" the Franko kid said.

"Shit!" the young Strubinger kid said.

A trio of the enemy razzed us, pointed at us, told us we were dead ("No shit, Sherlock," said the Strubinger kid), laughed at us, and moved on through the dense stalks.

The three of us brushed off the dry dirt and began to wipe off the dirty sweat that had turned to mud. Ugh indeed. We dejectedly began weaving our way back through the stalks, brushing and bitching as we went. "Shit!" the Strubinger kid said. "Ditto," the Franko kid said. "We'll get 'em na-na-next time," I said half-heartedly.

We cleared the stalks and trudged over to the side, to the edge of the open field. A half-dozen kids were sitting around in the hospital area, pretending they were nursing their wounds. Over in the cemetery lot, there were five corpses, some of the kids really getting into it, laid out stiff and straight, quiet as death, more quiet than they ever were in school. And off in the cornstalks, there was shouting and cursing and the occasional sound of a dirt grenade bursting.

"Pick a grave," the Franko kid said. Which we did.

We laid ourselves out in a neat line, flat on our backs, arms close in at the sides, like a line of used cars at the Rambler dealership.

For a long moment I closed my eyes and listened to the quiet — interrupted occasionally by the clash of war. I thought for a moment that we should protest the outcome. The first kids we came upon in the heart of the field had obviously started before the signal to begin. There was no way they could have gotten that far in such a short time. But then I gave that up and just lay quiet, watching the sky, watching the eagle or whatever it was circle high above.

I wished for a moment I was up there, flying. I frequently flew in my dreams, but in those dreams it wasn't easy. I had to launch myself from the ground and, unless I flapped my arms or something, I'd drift at exactly the same speed at which I'd launched myself. (If I had a rocket pack, like Commando Cody in the Saturday matinee serials, I could add speed to the drift, I thought.)

The bird circled, the sun was warm, the sounds of battle continued, but were steadily diminishing as the dead and wounded came in and took their places. I thought about the soldiers in *The Red Badge of Courage*, wandering around the edges of the battlefield, coming across rotting corpses — the dead eyes of the corpses staring at circling birds that would eventually descend to relieve them of those eyes.

Many of the fathers in town had been in service in World War II. Some had worked behind the lines or in training camps. My own father had trained troops in Panama before they were shipped out. Some of these fathers belonged to the VFW or the American Legion and they sat at the bar, drank their boilermakers, smoked unfiltered cigarettes, and talked, wistfully, about the war. It was the biggest thing that had ever happened to them, and they wanted to relive it over and over.

But some of the fathers had seen action. They'd shot at other men and had been shot at themselves. They seldom talked about it. My godfather had been a bombardier over Europe. I never heard him talk about the war.

I wondered if, in war, I'd be brave. Would I be a coward — or just an average guy who'd do the best he could to acquit himself well for his country and his buddies? I wondered, too, what it was like to really be dead. Maybe I'd circle the world like the black bird circling above us — or maybe I'd be like one bird in a flock of starlings, ESP-ing each upcoming turn so we'd all flow like a black cloud across the sky, synchronized with others in death like I had never been in life.

Another group of dead and wounded came in to join us — the honored dead and the Purple Heart recipients. The sounds of battle were diminishing. What little remained was now coming only every other minute or so.

The sun felt good. The young Strubinger kid speculated that the big black bird flying over us was a condor; of course he knew it wasn't, but he wished it were. Why not? Wishes don't cost anything. Besides, it was the kind of a day when anything was possible. When you could be killed in battle one minute, and thirty minutes later you could be up killing someone else — only to have them rise from the dead later and kill you back.

Jerry Strubinger strode up, full of himself. His side had four soldiers left; ours, all dead or dying. "Do we wanna keep the same teams or choose again?" he asked. We voted to keep the same teams; we'd reshuffle the players after lunch.

We all got up off the ground, brushed ourselves off, and prepared to go at it again — *eager* to go at it again. This time our team went behind the acre of cornstalks, and Jerry and his army stayed at the edge of the open field at the hospital and cemetery.

We decided on a new tack this time. Instead of splitting our army, we'd form a wedge and head directly into the corn, ready to overwhelm anything we encountered. It worked. Through the confusion of sidestepping cornstalks, we pushed our way through, mowing over the little patrols of enemy soldiers we encountered, losing only a few of our own, until we came out the other side, victorious, twelve live soldiers to their none.

Sweaty, breathing hard, dirty, we took a break, only to be interrupted by several mothers from the houses up above the fields, calling for their kids to come home. A dozen kids ran off to have lunch, while the rest of us bivouacked and tore into our bagged lunches, recounting, in heated and excited talk, some of the more memorable encounters with death and near-death we'd had over the previous two hours.

We lay on the grass, now neither wounded nor dead, just resting between battles (like Stephen Crane wrote they did). But it was warm and it was noon and not like the opening line of his book: "The cold passed reluctantly from the earth, and the retiring fogs revealed an army stretched out on the hills, resting." I rewrote the line in my head: "The warmth pressed sweetly on the earth, and the slowly sliding autumn shadows revealed an army stretched out on the field, resting."

The talk around me gradually lost its frenzy and trickled into mundane subjects like baseball and baseball card trades and comic books and school subjects. And somebody began to talk about the isthmuses and peninsulas they were studying in geography, and, for a time, the subject of war slid away.

Nobody asked Raymond Otto what his new used watch said about the time, because nobody wanted to be dictated to by a bunch of cogs and levers and artificial constraints. It was *now*, that's what it was. It had been now a few minutes ago and it would be now in a few minutes, but for today, it was always now — immediate time and no time at all. Maybe we napped, or dozed, or did that thing where you're between consciousness and slumber — floating about like a cloud or a circling bird.

Little by little, the home-lunch bunch began wandering back, and we lackadaisically got ourselves organized to go at it again inside the battle cage of the cornfield. We picked new sides, just like we would have done if we'd come back from lunch to play another ballgame. It didn't matter that the sides were much larger than a baseball team, or that there were girls and little kids sprinkled in. The same methodology of picking sides applied.

Drew and Aboo and I were on the same side this time. That was good. Drew and I worked well together, and Aboo lived just up the street and was very familiar with the cornfield. He was skinny as a string bean and could maneuver through the cornstalks as though there was nothing in his way. Some of the younger kids we got were decent, too. And the girls were eager to prove themselves in what was, for them, an unusual opportunity to forget playing with dolls and to mix it up with the boys and get dirty.

Jerry Strubinger took his army to the far side, and we staged our army once again in front of the hospital/cemetery. And in our huddle, we cooked up more of a guerrilla approach. Aboo would take a pair of the little fellas and two of the quicker girls and he'd head into the stalks to feign attacks, then they'd turn and run like hell, leading the enemy party directly into a trap. We'd set that up by concentrating the rest of our force into one impenetrable mass just inside the battlefield. We'd rise seemingly out of the very ground and wipe them out to the last soldier.

The strategy worked, too. Aboo was quick and smart and led his little scouting band well. He ghosted through the stalks, and the girls and the two young fellas were small and fast enough that they moved between the stalks with ease. They led one group of the enemy after the other into our trap, and pretty soon we had the hospital and cemetery filled. We all sprawled out after the battle ended, letting the sun heal our tiring legs, brushing off dirt that gradually dried, and comparing tactics.

The battles went until midafternoon. We could tell the day was moving away from us of its own accord in spite of the fact that we had put a hold on time. The sun crept toward the horizon and a cool breeze came up.

At one point, we were all propped up on our backs looking down the open field when Drew pointed out a figure running through the adjoining field, heading uphill toward South Street. "Ain't that Matt King?" he asked. "Where's he coming from?" Raymond Otto asked. A sour premonition began to infect our ranks like E. coli on a cruise ship.

"Looks like he's in a real hurry," one of the Franko kids said.

"He's an asshole," Jerry Strubinger observed. "Nobody wants to have anything to do with him."

"He's a real pariah," I said. (I'd waited weeks to find a suitable place to use that word. I'd read it in a Frank Yerby novel.)

One of the Franko kids snorted. "Yeah, ya get a bunch of 'em together in a stream 'en they'll eat the skin off yer bones, one little nibble at a time. I saw it on *Wild Kingdom.*"

"Wonder what he was doin' down there," Jerry said. "I don't trust that jerk. He couldn't have been up to any good." There were nods of agreement from among the ranks of the dead and wounded.

We lazily began to organize ourselves for yet another battle in the cornstalks. But this time it was taking us longer to roll up off the ground. We were gradually becoming sated with fun, as though it stuck to each of us like slabs of fat, making us heavy, making us work harder against the gravity pulling us back to Earth — like the hours after Thanksgiving dinner.

"We're keeping the same teams," Drew observed. "That was our plan."

"Yeah, OK," said Jerry as he gazed across the open fields below us.

Above us, a block away up on Third Street, there was some sort of ruckus. People were yelling back and forth to each other. Not kids — grown-ups. Then someone came running around the corner of the last house before the steps went downhill to The Swinging Bridge.

A moment later we heard the distant wail of a siren. It was coming from uphill, maybe from the fire station on Tenth Street. Its insistence rose and fell, carried and shredded by the slow breeze.

"What's going on?" one of the little kids from Fourth Street asked.

Drew pointed toward the tree line between us and The Swinging Bridge. Just topping the tree line was a wisp of white smoke. The big black bird began to soar in that direction, and two men came running down Third Street to the top of the steps, one of them pointing. They were excited. "Hurry up!" one of them shouted.

The wail of the siren grew louder. The dogs began to set up a howl. There was no doubt the fire truck was heading in our direction. More people milled at the top of the steps. One of the men yelled back to the gathering crowd: "Get a hose! Get some water!"

Drew pointed to the treetops where the white smoke was widening. He could have said "Fire!" but he didn't need to. As one, the three dozen kids took off at a sprint, crossing the field we were in, around the tree line and into the top of the open field. Then, as one, we stopped.

At the bottom of the field, at the northeast corner, our major-appliance-cardboard-box fort was in flames. They were vicious flames, like exhaust from an Atlas missile, but inverted — shooting straight up. About thirty feet above the ground, the bright red and yellow flames turned to white smoke. High above the flames, the black bird called out in alarm.

We began to move forward, as one, toward our fort, but by that time a fire engine — its lights spinning, its siren keening — had arrived at the top of the steps. Three firemen, in full firefighting regalia, were trying to unroll a hose and pull it down the steps. One of them had seen us closing in on the fire. "You kids! Stay away from the fire!" he shouted.

We stopped in our tracks, bumpety-bump, each at a different beat, acting as quickly or as sluggishly as each was likely to when ordered to do *anything* by someone in authority. We milled around, resisting, as best we could, the primal urge to go to the fire — restrained by the increasing number of adults either gathering at the top of the steps or running down to try to extinguish the blaze.

"That prick Matt King!" Catfish said. Matt King's grandmother lived directly across the street from Catfish and he was the one among us who had the most exposure to the suspected villain of the hour. "He burned our fort!" Fish's face contorted into a scowl. "I'll get him for this."

Of course, we all knew he wouldn't, at least not if Matt King made it safely back to his grandmother's. Many a time we'd pursued Matt King to his grandmother's house in hopes of paying him back in triplicate for one of his crappy stunts, only to be beaten back by his grandmother wielding her broom — like Mickey Mantle with a bat.

If the animosity against Matt King at that moment could have been canned, we'd have had to use oven mitts to handle it. Every one of us had comic books, model airplanes, sacks of marbles, trading cards, or other treasures in that fort. It was understood that anyone who wanted to could go there and play with anything, just as long as they, too, added something to the collective treasure trove. It was *all* gone — poof — up in flames.

The firefighters had finally wrestled their awkward hoses to the site, and they were spraying down the dry grass around the burning fort, hoping to keep the fire from spreading to the dead leaves at the base of the nearby trees. They were pretty much letting the cardboard fort burn itself out.

We mumbled and grumbled among ourselves, working up a lather like a lynch mob.

"Maybe we oughta get outa here," someone in the back of the mob suggested.

"Naw," Drew said sagely, "they already saw us here. They know who we are."

So we stood there, like a bunch of mutts, watching a year's worth of treasures go up in a pyre that emphatically marked the end of our extended summer. When it was all done and there wasn't even any smoldering left, and the crowd had burned out its enthusiasm, one of the firemen walked wearily up the hill to confront us. He was sweaty and out of breath. He held out his gloved hand. In the palm of it were a dozen damp cigarette butts. "Which of you smokes Chesterfields?" he demanded.

We looked around at each other, knowing full well that none of us did, but already anticipating the trouble each and every one of us would be in at the dinner table that night once our parents heard about this disaster.

"Matt King does," Jerry Strubinger offered.

The fireman looked us over. "Which one of you is Matt King?"

"None of us," Catfish said. "He lives down the street." He gave the fireman Matt King's grandmother's address.

"Our fort . . . " one of the little kids from Fourth Street began, on the verge of tears. "My baseball cards . . . "

"Nothing left," the fireman said. "Gone."

"I'm gonna get him." Catfish repeated.

The fireman shook his head. "No you won't. We'll take care of this." He pulled a notebook out of his pocket and, one by one, took down our names and addresses. On more than one occasion he'd mumble to himself, muttering the name of a father or mother he apparently knew personally. This was going to be bad — very bad.

"I don't want any of you leaving town," he said gruffly (and then smirked). "Understood?"

We indicated that we understood. "Where would we go?" one of the Franko kids started to ask.

"You'll go home now," the fireman said. Then he turned away and walked across the upper end of the field to join his fellow firefighters at the top of the steps.

"Shit," Jerry said.

"Double-shit," Drew said.

If the depth to which we had all plunged could be measured against the heights to which we'd flown earlier in the day, it would be similar to the distance from the Earth to the moon. But, other than mumbling, none of us said much else as we just fell apart like a ship on the rocks — heading off in clumps in different directions, off to our respective houses and our respective fates.

This definitely was not going to sit well with our parents. And that would hold true even if they caught Matt King and strung him up on the telephone pole on the corner of his grandmother's block. When a kid does something bad, especially *this* bad, there were repercussions for every other kid in town.

When we bumped into each other over the next few days, either coming out of church on Sunday or back in school on Monday, we compared notes. Different parents had different reactions, of course, but there seemed to be one universal theme: "I told you not to play with Matt King!" And one universal response: "We weren't."

We also heard that when the fireman went to confront Matt King's grandmother, she claimed he was with her all day.

What?

Helping her make brownies?

Doing homework?

His grandmother claimed that we were all a bunch of rotten barbarians trying to lay the blame for our bad deeds on her sterling grandson.

We didn't see much of Matt King after that. He was like a phantom; on occasion, we'd get a report or a glimpse. But, as with a phantom, there wasn't much substance to it.

Eventually, we all agreed that it had been one long and glorious day of war fought to the limit. It *was* one helluva wonderful day — a day, nevertheless, that went up in flames, as other glorious days in our lives probably would. (At least on some of those days, though, we would get to set our own fires.)

The Journalist's Life for Me

In the eighth grade, my cousin Dave Herman and I decided that what St. Joseph's School needed was a newspaper. This idea ran against common sense somewhat. You see, the eight grades that constituted St. Joe's were all contained in one building, and the grades, to some extent, intermingled each day — at morning and afternoon recess, at lunch, and on the way to and from school — so news traveled fast through the school by word of mouth if it was news worth spreading.

But we got our Idea off the ground, and here's why: Dave and I were sometimes indulged because our grandfather, Peter Herman, was the beloved janitor for the half-block complex of church, rectory, school, and nuns' residence. The nuns loved him and were consequently a bit lenient with us, his two eldest grandsons.

Dave and I never took any great advantage of this. We were both decent students, well-behaved and ambitious — always looking for something to do, some project to burn off the excess energy we had left after schoolwork, playing, reading, and performing the duties of altar boys.

(We also regularly helped Pop-Pop clean the school's classrooms over summer vacation, and we used push mowers to cut the grass at the church's cemetery in preparation for Memorial Day each year.)

As I've mentioned before, we were both altar boys (Knights of the Altar was the formal designation). But Dave and I were altar boys going in somewhat opposite directions. Any boy whose record was not festooned with a half-dozen felony convictions was expected to be an altar boy, serving God and the Church selflessly and with enthusiasm. (And it did take selflessness and enthusiasm to serve the early (5:15 A.M.) Sunday Mass, especially on snow days.)

Every altar boy was expected to be imbued with a special grace, a seed of wanting to serve society — more than the rest of mankind did. The nuns felt it their duty to water the seeds, in hopes that at least some of us would bloom and have The Calling — to become priests. The process was one that took great patience on the part of the nuns. All the seeds supposedly started out pretty much equal — all had potential (but, let's face it, not really). Along the way, the good nuns would weed out those who proved to have no real calling. Well, I was one of those weeds. I eventually found myself plucked from the lush garden of spiritual calling because I served a different god: baked goods.

From the time I was about nine years old, I'd been working Saturdays (and later, on weekday afternoons after school, too) delivering the baked goods of the Mauch Chunk Baking Company, under the direction of the unfiltered-Camel-smoking Shine Stermer, who serviced East Mauch Chunk from the back of a dark blue Chevy van. The job was one passed down through arcane methods from one neighborhood kid to the next. Two kids worked Shine's truck on Saturdays (a full eight-hour day, and sometimes more) and one of those two worked after school on weekdays. Every two years or so, the older of the two boys would move on to something more rewarding, like pumping gas and repairing tires. The remaining kid looked for someone about two years younger and knighted him to work as a partner on Saturdays — with the eventual sharing of weekday duties. To be The Chosen One was a great honor, because in those days a kid who had a regular job was seen by his peers as a sort of king.

I received the tap on the shoulder in a very odd way. I was sitting on the steps at the upper end of the park down below our house, at the narrow end where River Street joined South Street. I was sorting baseball cards into National and American Leagues, just minding my own business. From Center Street, the street where River and South joined, Francis W. "Cuzzy" Schweibinz ambled over. He lived on Second Street, between Center and North on the corner of School Street — an alley that led uphill to our school (on the lower side of Sixth Street) and the Bevin School (on the upper side of Sixth Street).

I certainly knew Cuzzy from playing sandlot baseball games and from his delivering baked goods to us and our neighbors on South Street, but we weren't close. He was two years older and much more sophisticated, so we moved in radically different circles. To him, I was just a snot-nosed kid.

In typical boy fashion, the whole deal lasted about two minutes, the way important things do (while unimportant things drag out to infinity — and beyond). Cuzzy explained that the kid who was his senior was moving on to higher-paying gigs, and that Shine needed a new junior baked-goods runner. As the remaining and now senior boy, Cuzzy got to pick who he wanted to bring on for the job. For some reason I (to this day) don't understand, he picked me for the position. Maybe he knew I was an expert on baked goods — at least when it came to eating them.

He explained that I'd start out working with him only on Saturday, an eight-hour shift — unless the weather got ugly, in which case we'd both be working until the route was completed. (And lordy, we did have some of those days that first winter, where the snow was up to the running board of the truck, and I'd be wearing my father's hip boots and running baked goods to snowed-in little old ladies.) "For the eight-hour shift, you'll make two dollars. Do you want the job or not?"

"Jeez! Well of course I want the job. But I gotta ask my parents if it's OK."

"OK then, you do that. Then let me know tonight, so if you can't do it I'll be able to get somebody else. If you *can* do it, be at my house at 7:00 A.M. Saturday."

"OK. I'll check. I'll be there."

"OK then. That's that." He sauntered off up the street, his business with me completed.

"Jeez! I'm about to be a working man," I thought to myself.

I shuffled my baseball cards together in no particular order and set off on a run to present the possibility of a career as a baked-goods runner to my parents. Naturally, they gave their OK. What were they going to say to the kid who got tapped for the sweetest job in town? The only stipulations from my parents were that I not let the job interfere with my homework and that I put half of my salary away toward my college education. (I refrained from pointing out that college was still eight years away — if we were all still alive, what with the Ruskies building up their stockpile of hydrogen bombs and all.) It was only Tuesday, but I got myself ready for Saturday morning.

The Saturday session — running baked goods to the houses of most of the people who lived on the east side of town — was heady stuff. I was employed. I wielded consumer power when it came to comic books, baseball cards, and sixteen-ounce Royal Crown sodas. And it got me out of the house and into an environment where I met a lot of nice people around town whom I would have never met otherwise.

On hot days, some of the ladies would come out on the porch to receive their baked goods, and they'd have a smile and a soda for me. At Christmas and Easter the bakery did up ethnic baked goods that were very popular with our Slovak and German customers. Quite a few customers were very generous at Christmastime, giving Cuzzy and me nice tips — sometimes homemade fudge and, at Easter, artistically rendered eggs and chocolate bunnies. Cuzzy and I were living the high life. Sure, we had to run baked goods in extremely hot weather and plow our way through new snow (up to our hips) from arctic storms. But we got along well.

And when Cuzzy resigned his position and moved on, I got to pick *my* junior partner. I picked my brother Drew, who adapted extremely well — to the point of going in to the bakery at 5:00 A.M. where he helped by loading the four route trucks before we went out with Shine.

There were some distressing things, however. For instance, we delivered baked goods to an elderly man who lived above his son's garage. When the son was home, he'd come out to get the baked goods. But when he wasn't, his father would toddle down the stairs. The old man was dying from cancer that was in the process of eating his face away, so he wore skin-colored patches over the ravaged portions of his face. He gave off an odor of death and rot. We felt sorry for him, but nobody we asked about him had any suggestions about anything that could be done to help him. He was doomed. And eventually he stopped coming down to meet us.

There was also the time that Drew ran the usual baked goods up to the front door of a rural customer who had grown tired of having kids and who had, just then, taken a shotgun to her pregnant abdomen to perform an abortion. Thanks to Drew's quick action, her life was saved, but the baby was lost.

While Cuzzy was still on the job, he eventually had me alternate with him on weekday after-school sessions. When my turn fell on a Thursday afternoon, it meant that I'd have to skip the weekly meeting of the Knights of the Altar. My absentee status every other week soon became a bone of contention with the nun who ran the club (and who regularly tried to nudge us to the priesthood).

She gave me an ultimatum. Either give up the silly job or give up being an altar boy. I countered; I didn't see why I had to attend Knights of the Altar meetings when I was quite capable of serving Mass just fine without being a card-carrying member of the Knights. No, she said. It was either-or. I checked with my parents and I checked with my grandfather, and they all agreed that the either-or approach was unfair, that a compromise would have worked in this case. But the good nun was adamant, so I became a working stiff and gave up any future as a priest.

My cousin Dave Herman continued being an altar boy and actually went off to the seminary after graduating from eighth grade at St. Joe's. Once he left, we used to correspond, but we wrote in code, just in case any of The Powers That Be were reading Dave's mail. (Heck, God already knew what we were writing about, since He could see through all codes and ciphers.) But Dave eventually dropped out of the seminary when he discovered he liked to be around girls a lot more than he liked to be around a mob of boys — and pious boys, at that.

Because we were the eldest of Peter Herman's grandchildren, Dave and I were not only allowed, but encouraged to pursue some of our harebrained schemes.

We put together ragged costumes appropriate to 1812 and the defenders of New Orleans and visited the lower classes. There we sang the Johnny Horton song "The Battle of New Orleans," which served as an intro for the teacher to go off on a fifty-minute spiel on the War of 1812. We were even allowed — no, encouraged — to bring to school knockoff versions of front-loading muskets. Imagine how that level of authenticity would go over in today's schools.

But our boldest move in the eighth grade — where being on the top of the school heap invested us with awesome powers — was to bring to St. Joe's our unique version of journalism, the publication of *St. Joseph's Spirit* (a spirit in more ways than one). It was run off on a spirit duplicator machine and to stand next to that contraption for too long, or to handle the still wet copies coming off the thing, was to suffer wooziness *in extremis* from the fumes of the raw, unadulterated alcohol.

Dave and I had read enough about the press to know that if you were really into it, you were said to have "printer's ink in your veins." In our case, we had "alcohol fumes in our lungs" — literally. To make matters worse, the machine was in a windowless closet with absolutely no ventilation — like the bottom of a caved-in mine. The best way to approach printing the newspaper was to take a deep breath, hold it, rush into the closet, turn the crank a few times, and retreat to gasp another breath of fresh air before repeating the process.

We weren't yet very good typists, so Sister Mary Albertus — the principal and our eighth-grade teacher — typed most of the articles. But it was our job to do the grunt work of gathering stories and cranking the printing machine. In order to make the newspaper a success, we talked two of our most able classmates — Larry Perin and Christine Mandracia — into working with us on the paper. Larry was editor (so he got out of having to close himself up in the spirit duplicator closet), Christine was news editor, I was sports editor, and Dave was manager. All four of us had one thing in common: between the four of us, we probably read twenty books a week. And now we were going to be published. Fantastic!

Dave and I had gone so far as to choose a newspaperman hero to emulate: we saw ourselves in the mold of John Wilkes, for whom nearby Wilkes-Barre was named. He was a fiery English journalist whose campaigns against the king and others kept his household expenses down (by keeping him in hot water). We downplayed the fact that John Wilkes Booth had been named after him (and that they were distantly related).

The first issue, dated "Sept., October, Nov., 1959" was all of two sides of one page. The hard-hitting, groundbreaking new rag on the block broke such stop-the-presses stories as "Improvements at St. Joseph's." This article gave details of the newly remodeled seventh- and eighth-grade classrooms on the second floor, told that the first grade had been moved from the basement to the first floor and that their old classroom was going to be changed into a library, and reported that there were new bulletin boards in all the classrooms. Wow!

The Honor Roll for each class was also listed on the front page and continued around to the second page. On the second page, there was an update of the money the classes had raised for the Catholic missions to help them convert the poor pagans around the world. (Our school had been able to convert $278.43 worth of pagans.)

The newspaper was popular enough that a second issue was launched. This one moved to a bi-monthly schedule rather than quarterly and doubled in size—two sheets of paper, printed on both sides and stapled in the upper-left-hand corner. We also began giving bylines on some of the stories. Joanne Mormak reported on Ann Biank and Christne Mandracia winning the spelling bee. Christine, in turn, reported on progress in the appeal to collect broken or damaged rosaries that would be repaired and sent to converts in foreign lands.

A little humor column called "Whisperings from the Wings" was introduced. Example: When Sister Marie James, the fourth-grade teacher, asked for three large cities in the state of Pennsylvania, the pupil's response was Philadelphia, Pittsburgh, and *Nesquehoning*. (Ba-dum-bump!) And in a flagrant mismanagement of academic integrity, all four newspaper editors made the Honor Roll. (Time for some investigative reporting to get to the bottom of that.)

On the missionary front, our school was up to converting $401.24 worth of pagans in foreign countries. (Our local pagans were apparently on their own.) There were reports on Knights of the Altar meetings and a special privilege of the choir to sing at the annual Solemn High Mass celebrating the Circumcision of Our Lord.

The second issue was obviously a roaring success, and everyone old enough to read looked forward to the next issue, which would no doubt be bigger and better than ever. Unfortunately, there was no third issue.

Apparently imbued with the spirit of John Wilkes and muckrakers past and future, I personally killed *St. Joseph's Spirit* when, as sports editor, I wrote an editorial critical of the way the basketball coach picked the team — giving too much weight in the process to his own son.

Filled with righteous pride in a job well done — rooting out evil and corruption wherever it might abide — I turned in my incisive screed to Sister Mary Albertus. A few hours later, I was asked to take a walk across the school grounds to the rectory where I was to meet with the assistant pastor. Sister Albertus indicated that the meeting had to do with the recently submitted editorial. No doubt the editorial's persuasive argument had swayed the assistant pastor, and he wanted to confer over what could be done to correct this case of runaway nepotism.

We lowly students were seldom received in the rectory. That was sacred ground for only the priests and the most holy of adults. I knocked on the door and the housekeeper answered. I blurted out my business and she had me sit in a stuffed chair in the front room. The room was spotless and tastefully decorated, but it looked a bit sterile — sort of like our front parlor, where everything was situated just so, but nobody was allowed to enter except on Christmas and Easter. There were muffled sounds coming from deeper within the rectory. There was no music playing and no telephones rang. (In those days, a ringing telephone usually meant something bad had happened.)

Father Zigley, the assistant pastor, came in looking grave and solemn, as though someone has just died. (I'd heard no telephone ring.) He held my scathing editorial in his hand as though it was, indeed, too hot to handle. He sat down across from me, and for the next five minutes tried to explain his adult rationale for why this was not a good thing that I had done. The only part I remembered later was about how the basketball coach was a volunteer, his time was valuable, and we should respect our elders.

When Father Zigley was through with me, he asked if I had anything to say. I didn't. He showed me to the door and I walked the long mile or two across the asphalt playground to the school. He didn't return my editorial; he probably placed it in my permanent file. Nothing else was said about the school newspaper, either. It was allowed to die a quiet death. The third issue, which would have been the February/March 1960 edition, never came out.

By that time, spring was blossoming all over the place, and everyone's mind was on the warming weather and the momentum of the school year rushing to a finish. We seniors were thinking in terms of our class trip to Dorney Park. The once-popular newspaper faded from the minds of the student body, and nobody (that I knew of) so much as suspected that I'd been responsible for its death.

The concept of the newspaper didn't fade from my mind, however. The publishing high fueled by the spirit duplicator's alcohol-rich vapors had taken hold. Within the next few years, the publishing devil would take the form of science fiction fanzines, and, in the process, I'd graduate to sloppy, inky mimeograph machines.

Cashiered out of the Knights of the Altar, guilty for the death of a very nice school newspaper, I was getting ready to move still further away from the lower end of East Mauch Chunk. High school loomed and my parents had declared that the choice of attending public or Catholic high school was entirely up to me. Of course, if I chose Catholic high school, it involved a fifteen-mile bus ride every day, and there went my lucrative bakery delivery job.

Decisions, decisions. In the end, I'd make the easy decision and stay close to home (remember, geography) and close to the kids I knew and had grown up with. But I'm getting ahead of myself. I hadn't graduated from eighth grade yet, and with the number of people at St. Joe's who were becoming unhappy with me, I might never *pass* the eighth grade. I might get thrown out on my ear.

Tangled Tongue

When the average person is asked to rate the scariest thing a human being can do, it overwhelmingly involves public speaking. Take the most talkative person you know and push him or her out in front of an audience of five hundred and there is often a deafening silence.

In Catholic grade school, we were regularly required to haul our sorry selves from our carefully lined-up desks, stand up straight, and recite or read out loud. A few members of my class actually seemed to thrive on the ordeal. But most of us didn't. In typical, strict-parochial-grade-school fashion, everyone had an assigned seat, based on how your last name fell in the alphabet, and all recitations or readings followed the same rigid order. So we sat and waited, with tropical armpits, like a line of rebel fighters put up against a wall to be shot — by an executioner with a slow-loading musket.

Much like the rising of the sun each day, like the change of the seasons, like the tides that lapped the shore, the sequence of recitation was chiseled in stone — in this case, on your tombstone. The only way to avoid the inevitable was to get yourself sick that day. But that would only delay things a little, because special consideration would be made for your sickly self on your first day back. That's when you would get to start off the session.

It is anecdotally proven that a person who is suffering in the extreme, even if it involves something bloodless like public speaking, will sometimes exit that poor lump of clay for a time to stand outside the suffering — and watch. It is a matter of survival. On numerous occasions, I've had that experience. It is not unlike the drifting above one's own corpse that is described by "out-of-body" travelers, although the floating above in this case is cheapened — it's more a standing next to. It ain't the same thing. The instance of "being beside myself," as I used to call it, that sticks most tenaciously in my mind is the time in the sixth grade when I became hung up on the word *the* for nearly fifteen minutes during a reading-aloud session that turned into a long, cold, lonely century.

I'd been a stutterer since age five, and with diligent practice, I had become very good at it, but on that day I far surpassed even my wildest expectations. The terrible trio of letters required to construct the word *the* became stuck in my throat like a treble hook, the barbs anchoring themselves more firmly the harder I fought them, pinching at first, gouging eventually, drawing blood when I bit the inside of my cheek during one frantic attempt to be over with it. But no tactic I marched out from the extensive cornucopia of devices would free me from the sharp steel hooks.

I backed up a few words in the text, hoping to get a fresh running start that would give me the momentum I'd need to crash through *the*, but each time I rushed toward the word, the fishing line would go taut and I'd be pulled up short, my jaw vibrating like a chainsaw in need of a tune-up, buckets of water pouring down my sides from my wellspring armpits. The sound of classmates behind me rolling their eyes became deafening, and the big, plain, round clock at the front of the class above the blackboard sent the second hand toward the next black tick mark at the pace of rust.

Because everyone had their books open in front of them and could plainly see what the next word was supposed to be, I was cut off from falling back on the veteran stutterer's most used stratagem: synonyms. The fact that the English language is so incredibly rich is, I think, a balm for the stutterer. The language literally drips with synonyms, every one of which is held in the regard of a high sacrament from heaven by those of us with tangled tongues.

When a stutterer becomes hung up on the word *postpone*, he can slip over it and banish its sorry butt by substituting the word *delay*. Even if he already started off with the *pa-pa-P* sound, literally everyone wants to move on, and will overlook the fact that P got deep-sixed and D was recruited. But with the day's reading sitting in front of each one of my classmates like tombstones lined to the horizon, the entire brilliant universe of synonyms had blinked out.

Now, because this was 1958, because this was small-town America, because this was a strict Catholic grade school, and because the nun/teacher had a firm sense of what was right and wrong, the Lord was going to stop the world in its orbit until either I finished my reading out loud or the clock mercifully helped the period run itself out; and everyone in class was going to be an accomplice — willing or not — in this torture. Looking back at it decades later, I believe my teacher did the right thing. Even standing up next to my desk that day, I knew she was doing the right thing. Her insistence meshed with my own genetic stubbornness to get the job done, no matter how painful to myself and others. But *that* stubbornness at *that* point was an emotion — and it was an emotion taken nearly to the extreme — where it mixed with an army of other emotions that marched back and forth while I stood gnawing away on the fishing line leader. I was stubbornly, angrily, nervously, anxiously hoping to bite through it. Then *the*, with pieces of my tortured flesh on its barbs, could be spat out onto the floor and the world could again be allowed to spin.

After enough minutes had passed, after I'd backed up a dozen times to make a fresh run at that damned word, the attempt slid into a nearly dormant phase where I continued to try to break loose, but no longer tried with all my might. Like a fish, I was tiring. While some of the energy I had left was diverted to lift me, for a while, away to the side and a bit above the embarrassing exhibition to which I was now only marginally connected, I began to float a few inches off the floor, next to my mortal, suffering, stupid self.

I looked down at *me*, analyzed and recorded everything — apart, as though I were merely an observer, another bystander. I watched the heads of my classmates, watched the chin perched on the knuckles, elbow planted firmly on top of the desk. I watched one of the girls — who actually liked to read aloud — watching me with an interest I interpreted as encouragement, as though she were trying to will me through that *the*, or to lend me one of her fluid, flawless versions of *the*.

That sterling reader was Christine Mandracia, who, I believe, was born in a library. She devoured books the way some of us gulped penny candy. She probably had a holster filled with library cards the way some of us had gunbelts filled with fake .44 caliber bullets. And, boy oh boy, could she read out loud! We began to think she never slept, but instead, after reading her daily fill of a dozen books, stayed up all night practicing the next day's reading. When she did sleep, it must have been with a dictionary salted away under her pillow so she could absorb, by osmosis, dozens of additional words. She was a word junkie and there was no word that fazed her.

I can still remember the first time I heard Christine utter the word *naiveté*. I could figure from its context in the sentence what it meant, and that was made easier by the fact that in her reading, she had never even so much as paused in her approach. There was no wall, no speed bump, not even a fly speck in her way as that exotic word flowed out as merely part of a sentence, where it lay quivering, not so much defeated as simply not taken seriously. Wow!

The good Sister of Christian Charity (I've forgotten her name) sat in the front at her wide desk with a nearly beatific smile on her face, as though she were privileged to have a box seat at the killing of St. Stephen, ecstatic as each arrow pierced his tender flesh.

I floated while my lowly body stubbornly embarrassed itself, choking on the fish hooks. Meanwhile, I could pick out, around the class, several classmates who secretly appreciated what I was doing for them — because the longer I hung up there, the more the class droned on, and the less chance there'd be that they'd have to get up and read that day.

When I finally returned to my body, it was with a sense of disgust and self-loathing. I was *still* stuck on one of the most used of all words in the English language, a word so well-used that the edges should have long ago been worn off of it. But here I was, still impaled on the three little hooks, beaten, humiliated by a word a toddler or a moron could use every day without even thinking about it.

The mundane fact of a word's simplicity, I had discovered, was the obstacle stutterers tripped themselves up on. Regular people don't waste time and effort *thinking* about the act of speaking — it's just something they *do*. Of course, some people are more adept at speaking without thinking than others, while stutterers never are. When the regular person has something to say, the regular person assembles the necessary words in as logical an order as possible and they flow out of the mouth. But where the regular person doesn't even *think* about the mechanical act of speaking, the stutterer thinks of little else. The stutterer thinks about sentences that aren't scheduled to trip him up for hours or days to come. (I use the pronoun *him* here to identify the stutterer, not just because it is traditional to use the male pronoun unless the gender is known, but also because four or five times as many boys take up the stuttering trade.)

It is this anticipation of stuttering, based upon a history of having stuttered before, that assures that there will always be more stuttering to come. Simply put: What's practiced in the head is realized in the world. Which is why, when they forget to work on their stuttering, stutterers forget to stutter. Shorty's opinion was that if I could be caught on occasion not stuttering, and he'd actually overheard me doing just that, then I could and should be able to speak fluently all the time (and I was therefore stuttering for an ulterior reason). He was convinced that I was simply trying to call attention to myself, and I should goddamned find some other way of doing that.

This argument, of course, completely overlooked the plain and obvious fact that during the act of stuttering, the stutterer would prefer to be in Zanzibar strung up by his thumbs, or anywhere else in the world, or even on some other world, than where he is at the moment — stuttering.

So, what caused me to take up this hated habit and perfect it to such an extent?

It was not a profession that was unique among my peers. In our class, four of us were stutterers — two part-time, the other two, accomplished practitioners. Catfish Gavornick and Richie Guman (the undertaker's son) tried it out, but couldn't manage to stick with it, and by the fourth grade gave it up. Bob Kmetz — a kid as fat as a skeleton, literally an Adam's apple attached to a stick, a kid who'd been kept back a grade and was prone to anger when his affliction began to get away from him — stuck with his stuttering and became rather accomplished at it.

My inclination to take on the stuttering art was instigated at age five when I got my tonsils taken out, as you've already heard. I "practiced" and "perfected" my stuttering in the months following that twice-under-ether tonsillectomy. Of course, during the first, second, and third grades, when we were all trying out our stuttering, my father insisted that I was copying — imitating the others — and I should just give it up or he'd make sure I gave it up. I never did. He never did, either.

Prior to that, I'd had the typical fumbling with the language that anyone who's attempting to put together an intelligible sentence or two would have. I began to speak early and had a few mishaps along the way. (I used to call a *bus* a *bis*.) But eventually, it seemed I sorted this all out, much like everyone else my age did.

But following The Incident at Tonsil Creek, my speech deteriorated, helped along by my father's growing insistence that I was a weakling and coward for stuttering — modified, later, to a firm belief that I was doing it for no other reason in the whole wide world than to make *his* life miserable. Poor Shorty — another in a long line of personal setbacks.

The stuttering problem was further aggravated when I went to school. I was inclined to favor the regimented structure of a Catholic school. (Are we first-borns predictable, or what?) I liked the neat regularity of classes, and I enjoyed *most* of it because there were lots and lots of books involved. But I lived in constant fear at school — probably because the prime engine of motivation and discipline there, at least as I saw it, was *fear*.

The rules were very simple and easy to keep in mind: Do what you're told or you'll have the yardstick taken to you, and then you'll go to Hell. This basic rule of cause and effect was augmented by another: If you are beaten in school for something you did or didn't do, when you get home your father will beat you doubly bad.

I was very well-behaved at school. (Are we first-borns predictable, or what?) I was a model student, but like the too-often whipped dog, I lived in fear of making a mistake and receiving the consequences. Of course, such fear worked wonderfully to trigger the stuttering, which in turn was aggravated not only by fear of the teachers above me, but of ridicule from my fellow students around me. My fellow students — children all — could be cruelly insensitive. (I am constantly provoked to near nausea by the total ignorance of adults who refer to children as little angels. There is no crueler animal in the forest than a kid who smells blood. Did these adults get to skip childhood or something?)

By the sixth grade, my fellow students had settled in to a certain boredom with my stuttering. I'd spent six years getting them used to it; they knew what to expect. And for a pack of kids who lived for the next potential victim to come stumbling naively down the jungle trail, how much mileage can the dumb ones get out of imitating a stutterer, then adding, "NAA na-na-na-NAA!"?

We had already been through all the basic meanness back in the first grade. I didn't get into fights over the teasing. I just stood there and took it, like I did at home — tears spilling out, but too stubborn to make a run for it. Besides, as with all the other double-edged swords my father had fashioned for me, there was this one: He wanted me to be a man and stand up for myself (but certainly not against *him*) but at the same time didn't want me fighting at school, or he'd teach me what a good whuppin' was all about. So I stood and took it until: a.) a nun walked by and broke it up, b.) some sympathetic kids broke it up, or c.) the jerk who was doing it got bored and wandered off to look for more interesting prey.

Unfortunately, what started as taunting ("Ha-ha-hey, Mushmouth. What ya sa-sa-say?"), escalated once the uncontrollable tears began to slip out: "Crybaby! Crybaby! Mommy's boy is cryin'!" This, of course, tended to draw a crowd of the rudderless. Kids who weren't sure they wanted to get on another kid's case because he stuttered weren't as reluctant to get on a kid's case if he was standing there crying like a leaky fire hydrant. To be fair, it should be noted that — at the age of six or seven or eight — this sort of behavior has an enviable gender-blindness. Little girls are ready, willing, able, and sometimes even more eager than boys to join in against the goat-of-the-moment.

One of the aspects of the stuttering lifestyle that is most unfair is that, by its nature, it sets you up for failure. One of the greatest stumbling blocks to fluent speech is frequently the stutterer's own name. (I've learned, from therapists who spend entire careers studying this, that this blocking on your own name is a symptom of self-loathing — your own name being the reminder of that self-loathing which triggers the stuttering and the subsequent feelings of inadequacy and self-loathing.)

I thought about changing my name to something easier, but theoretically, as long as I associated myself with my name, with any name I gave myself, it would eventually come back to bite me. Since a stutterer has such a difficult time with his own name, it tends to be more than a bit difficult mixing and socializing. When you know that the first thing expected out of your mouth is an introduction: "Ha-ha-hello. Ma-ma-ma-my na-na-name is Ra-ra-ra . . . hey, ya got fifteen minutes to spare?"

My father stood firm on his knowledge that I was stuttering just to get attention. Since I didn't stutter all the time — he'd heard me occasionally speak fluently, god dammit — I could turn it off and on at will. Consequently, there was no reason to try to go out of his way to get help for his first-born son.

My mother felt otherwise. By second grade, she engaged the services of an elderly woman whose name I don't recall, who came on Saturday mornings when I'd much rather have been out playing, and we sat in front of the vanity mirror in my parents' bedroom. She had me read, out loud, the funny pages from the previous Sunday's newspaper — funny pages that I'd read and memorized six days earlier.

I sympathize with kids who are required, by strict parents with big dreams for their offspring, to go to music lessons on Saturday mornings. The primary difference between them and myself was that, while their skill with a musical instrument improved and someday they'd likely perform in front of an audience, my speech continued to stick to its principles with an eye toward my voluntarily turning myself into a mute. Even if the budding musicians eventually gave up their lessons, they would, at parties twenty years down the road (with a few drinks onboard), very likely give in to the urgings of their fellow party-goers to sit down and bang out a few Broadway tunes on the piano. Who wants to hear someone recite the words in the comic-strip balloons of twenty-year-old Sunday funnies?

In my attempts to control words instead of being manipulated by them, the inside of my mouth occasionally got chewed up — from biting my tongue and the inside of my cheek until my mouth felt the way a pound of ground round looks.

After six months of futile attempts to affect a cure, the well-meaning elderly lady stopped coming. I had made literally no progress and may have managed to get worse. It's difficult to speak fluently when you're talking around a mouthful of raw cheek. I hadn't been miraculously cured; of course, my father credited it to my incurable stubbornness. He was correct about my stubbornness; it was what pushed me to continue to fight *against* stuttering. But in that fighting against stuttering I was fighting against myself. Consequently, I had a formidable opponent.

But as far as stubbornness went, once Dorothy squirted me out, my father was relegated to the bush leagues. When he'd come after Drew and me, Drew would hightail it out of there as fast as his legs could carry him. He knew he'd get his punishment later, and didn't mind. Perhaps he kept betting that Shorty would forget he owed Drew a whupping. Shorty never did. I, on the other hand, would stand my ground, take my beating, and then — that fatal flaw over which I had no control — I'd begin to cry. Not a whimpering or howling or sobbing cry, it was just big tears welling up and rolling down to splatter the well-waxed kitchen linoleum. And, of course, that would set Shorty off even more. (My brother missed this predictable escalation of Shorty's rage. Maybe Drew was smarter than I thought.)

The whole scenario became as boring as a skip on a record: "I'll knock your stubborn streak out of you!" To approximate the performance, you've got to clench your teeth and make the veins on your forehead and neck stand out prominently. Huff yourself up like a pissed-off pit bull and growl: "Now I'll give you something to cry about!" Now say this, *with feeling*: "Get out of my sight. You're no son of mine, crybaby. Go to your room!" Close with an aside to Dorothy: "Don't give him supper tonight!" (Every once in a while that last bit worked to my advantage, especially on nights when we were having fried liver and onions. Besides, I kept Hershey bars cached under my mattress.)

During the sixth and seventh grade, I used to leave school early on Tuesday and Thursday afternoons and take the bus across town to the Immaculate Conception Catholic School (the Irish-Catholic parish), where a traveling nun with some speech therapy background visited to work with the defectives like myself. She had more success than the dear elderly lady who had me read funny papers I'd already read, but it did little to improve my speech. In fact, it was under her reign that I set my record on the word *the*, which, in retrospect, I might still be stuck on if the clock hadn't ended the period.

After eighth grade, St. Joseph's School ran out of grades, and we had to make a decision to either go to the local public high school or get bussed to the regional Catholic high school, Marian High. I chose Jim Thorpe Area Junior-Senior High School, and almost immediately was shuttled off three lunch hours a week to speech therapy with a handful of other special education kids, several of whom were making giant strides toward a life of crime.

Our "special–ed" classroom was the dead area behind the back curtain of the stage in the auditorium where there was a prop sofa and a table and a half-dozen folding chairs. There's not much to be said about those hour-long sessions. Not much happened on a fairly regular basis, except that one guy, who wore a black leather jacket with chains and engineer boots, talked back to the therapist a lot, was truant as often as possible, and claimed to have no goddamned stuttering problem in the first place. Since I knew — from my own experiences hiking and loitering with the South Street Gang — what kind of knife the bulge in his back pocket represented, I agreed with him. I told him I didn't think he should be there. He thanked me for my support and attempted to curse the therapist, but got badly hung up on "Ba-ba-ba-ba-bii-bii-bitch!" and left.

I'm left with two thoughts concerning stuttering, and I stress that they are, very simply, my personal feelings and not the conclusions of experts.

1.) Once a stutterer, always a stutterer. I think that, like alcoholism, once you work hard enough to establish what you are, you are that for life. Normal, regular people sometimes stutter, but aren't stutterers, just like normal, regular people sometimes drink too much and get falling-down drunk, but aren't necessarily alcoholics. Once a stutterer, no matter how fluent you become over the years, you are still a stutterer. You've been intimate with a problem that has shaped you and that continues to influence your sense of identity. And in the back of your mind, you know you could resume the behavior at any moment.

2.) Some years ago, a group condemned Porky Pig as a cartoon character who undermines the self-esteem of stutterers. Allow me to point out that the group speaks for itself; it does not in any way speak for this stutterer or for several stutterers with whom I've discussed this matter.

You just keep on doing what you've been doing, Porky. As far as some of your fellow stutterers are concerned, you are the only positive role model in all of cartoondom. You aren't violent, destructive, mean, evil-spirited, conniving, crass, base, or any of those things that so many cartoon characters are.

Yes, Porky Pig is an OK guy as far as this stutterer is concerned. And as for Porky's undermining the self-esteem of stutterers, Porky Pig exudes self-esteem, good fellowship, and a bright outlook on life, and he doesn't carry a blade in his back pocket. If we can't measure up in life with a stutter, it's our fault, not Porky's. So there.

Gallant Knights and Their Ladies

Sex is not a four-letter word.

During our childhood, it was a million-word novel with a Schlage lock securing the covers so they could never be opened. That way, the secrets of sex could never be glimpsed or contemplated — forget about them being experienced.

Our parents never spoke of it. Television seldom hinted at it. In fact, the possibility that Ozzie and Harriet Nelson enjoyed a sexual attraction to one another was made laughable by the fact that they were required (by television censors) to sleep in separate beds. How David and Ricky came to be was open to speculation. Maybe they came from Central Casting.

In grade school, we wore uniforms that effectively disguised any hint of sexuality, while the good nuns made it emphatically clear: If you think of sex, you'll go to Hell; if you engage in sexual activity, you'll go to Hell; and if you touch yourself "down there," first of all it will fall off, then you'll go blind, and *then* you'll go to Hell.

Conclusion: If, as a result of all of those possibilities — or, rather, of any one of them — you'll go to Hell, it might be best to just rush past the thinking about sex and the near occasion of sex and get right down to the real thing, because you're going to Hell anyway. We knew all about Sodom and Gomorrah from Bible history class, so we could only conclude that those cities were marched out in front of us as an enticement to consider doing bad stuff, to test our mettle in the Sin Wars.

Sex, if you were married, was not only all right, but actually required — only for the purpose of producing children, however. Hence, all of us counted the number of kids various parents had and multiplied by one to arrive at an estimate of how many times they'd had sex.

Since the lower end of South Street was dominated by boys and one of the only girls — Patsy Bronko — was a tomboy, the mystery of girls wasn't exactly an in-your-face thing on a daily basis. Catfish Gavornik's parents had a girl after they had him, but you didn't view your buddy's sister as a girl. She was just his kid sister — a whole different species from girls.

The one girl of note on our block, Kitty Carrigan, sort of didn't count because she was a few years older, always wore dresses, and never played with any of us. She moved in a whole different world than real kids did.

Our awareness of girls jumped when we went to first grade; our grade was roughly half boys and half girls. Whatever strange chemicals had affected the parents on lower South Street to make mostly boys apparently didn't extend beyond our couple of blocks. In first grade, the girls were seated on one side of the room and the boys on the other, and that was just fine with us. The nuns didn't even need to take pains to keep us apart, because we had nothing in common with each other.

The first grade boys weren't exactly members of the Little Rascals' He-Man Woman Haters Club. We didn't need to join a club for that. Hell, nature took care of creating the boundaries. We were a bunch of miniature barbarians! Ring the recess bell and it was like half-a-room full of Pavlov's dogs. The most trouble the poor nun had was to hold the boys back at the recess bell so that the girls could exit the classroom first. For our part, it was explained to us over and over again, this was "being a gentleman" (whatever that was). If a girl dawdled on her way out the door to recess, she was likely to get run down by the stampede of boys on their way to play stickball or tag or dodge ball.

We certainly knew that girls were different from us. Their uniforms proved it. We boys wore blue trousers, white shirts, and blue ties. The girls wore white blouses and blue skirts. When the regimen of the classroom gave way to recess, the girls tended to stick together in groups like blood clots — while the boys tended to explode like the balls on the break shot in a game of pool. Thank goodness the good nuns were much more intuitively astute than the boneheads involved in elementary education today. The nuns realized that boys and girls were born different. We were wired differently, acted differently, and thought differently (when we thought at all).

We had recess in the morning, at lunch break, and in the afternoon — three times during the school day when the boys could blow off steam so they could return to class relatively docile. We had thirty-six kids in our class and none of them had ADD. Our parents and the nuns had taught us to be disciplined, to behave, and to exhibit a modicum of self-control. If we lapsed, we knew there were consequences, and we accepted those consequences — which, of course, included corporal punishment.

The nuns had long since forsaken the free wooden yardsticks (provided by Marzen's Hardware Store at the start of each school year) in favor of the expensive but durable yardsticks with the metal edge. Those of us who never misbehaved enough to get hit probably suffered as much as the kid in the next desk who was getting it. The yardstick was such an effective tool, eventually it had only to be displayed to serve its purpose.

Was there any overt sex education? Well, unlike today's kids, we never got to see one of our teachers struggle to put a rubber on a cucumber. Occasionally, in the later stages of our grade-school careers, the class would be divided by gender and the assistant pastor would spend an hour with the boys talking about matters of sexuality he thought appropriate, while the nun would lecture the girls. (I'm not sure how effective that was — being told about sex by two people who weren't allowed to have any.)

There was increasing sexual tension as we grew up. We had discipline; we wore uniforms; our teachers were strict. But you can't turn a knob and shut off the boiling, bubbling juices of neo-adolescence. The whole process just begins to happen on its own, and you're either its slave or its keeper.

What would be the ultimate undoing of our class was the simple biological fact that girls mature, physically and psychologically, much earlier than boys. On the playground, several of the girls could outrun us, and as we would learn, we were going to spend our years at St. Joe's always a few steps behind them.

Besides being naïve, many of the boys would have their lives complicated by the fact that they were also romantics. A girl could get away with hitting a boy, but a boy was never to hit a girl. Girls were to be revered because they existed on a higher plane. We were taught that explicitly. But we also learned it on Saturday mornings when we went to the library and sat in the little kids' annex and paged through picture books of the Knights of the Round Table and read tales of Robin Hood and Maid Marian. Some years later the whole "knights" thing would come back to preoccupy a handful of us stupid romantic boys.

We did have puppy-love romances in grade school. From the second grade onward, although I wasn't a bigamist, I had a heavy thing for Ann Haggerty *and* for Annette Funicello. Ann Haggerty was in my class while Annette (only one name was necessary — this, long before Cher or Madonna or any of the come-lately celebrities) was, well, the object of desire for exactly 35,471,230 boys around my age. Yeah, that would amount to roughly 94.6% of all Baby Boomer boys. Pulled in on our cable-assisted TV sets every weekday, *The Mickey Mouse Club* provided a window through which we could be voyeurs on the blossoming adolescence of the lovely (and later voluptuous) Annette. The rumor that she was dating that Canadian twit Paul Anka was devastating news to a generation of American boys.

But let's be honest: our youthful priorities were totally screwed up. The chemicals that coursed through our veins made us raving morons.

Gabe Kaplan, the creator of *Welcome Back, Kotter*, has a comedy album in which he does a routine about nocturnal emissions. He stresses the cluelessness of a young boy the first time it occurs. A combination of "What the hell was that?" and "How do I get it to happen again?" He also jokes about how young boys are suddenly eager to save their mothers work by offering to do their own laundry, especially the bedsheets. He's right on the mark in that regard.

With no parental warning that some dark night I would be the hapless victim of a "wet dream," I tiptoed down the hallway to the bathroom, avoiding the boards in the floor that creaked, and came back with a glass of warm water, which I used to clean up the mess, spending the rest of the night sleeping on one-third of the bed. And, of course, feeling betrayed by a body that I increasingly didn't understand or recognize. And, as you can imagine, feeling dirty and guilty because I'd slipped over one more wet cobblestone on the highway to Hell. (I hadn't touched myself down there. It had gone off on its own. Unlike a gun, it apparently had no safety catch.)

As strange desires rose, we became increasingly confused. Not only was no one telling us what to expect, but, as boys, we were not inclined to go into a long discussion with anyone about a malady that we were sure affected only us. The evil desires were not easily subdued by a cold bath, either. They were merely driven underground — or in my case, into the attic, where they found paper kindling to stoke the fire.

When my sisters came along, starting when I was eight, Drew and I were moved to the attic — the second floor bedrooms were given over to Kathleen and Barbara. The attic was unheated and was not insulated. It was a hotbox in the summer and an icebox in the winter. At the eastern end of the attic, where the roofline slanted downwards, there was a storage area where my mother stored Christmas decorations and various things that were used on a seasonal basis.

Also stored there were the army manuals Shorty had pilfered from the military when he left. And there were a couple of boxes of books. In one of the boxes was an art book that included a full-page, four-color reproduction of *The Naked Maja* by Goya, a picture I soon memorized. I tried to convince myself that it was a work of art, not a near occasion of sin. I thought about becoming an art curator, but was dissuaded by some of the abstract art in the same book.

Among the books was a pile of paperbacks with lurid covers showing women in dire circumstances: a comely young dark-haired woman in a tight yellow dress menaced by a Japanese colonel, a damsel in a dark metropolitan neighborhood menaced by a guy in a dark-colored trenchcoat, a cowgirl menaced by a pair of wild Indians, etc. I don't remember the titles, but I do remember the covers.

Then there were the now defunct men's adventure magazines that my father brought home from work at the Bethlehem Steel Company. Magazines with titles like *For Men Only* ("Special Book Bonus: I Ruled A Pagan Kingdom"), *Man to Man Yearbook* ("For What Would You Sell A Woman?"), *True Action* ("The Day The Panzers Raided France's City Of Beautiful Women"), and *Untamed* ("I Crashed The Bordello For Millionaires Only"). There were dozens of titles, but they would soon become extinct thanks to *Playboy* and the army of *Playboy* knock-offs that turned men's magazines into "slicks." It was the transitional era between our father's generation and our own.

Shorty's magazines often had World-War-II-themed covers: a group of doughty GIs being beaten and tortured by a bevy of beautiful Nazi babes wearing lacy bras and panties and swastika armbands, or a lovely young woman in bra and panties being menaced by a leering Japanese colonel wanting to do unspeakable things to her. (That Japanese guy really got around.) Other covers showed adventures that called for a big, strong, heroic man to save the day — maybe a scantily-clad young woman wading through a piranha-choked stream, being pursued by a frenzied tribe of South American cannibals. You get the idea.

To date, I had acted upon nothing, but was increasingly assaulted by temptation — from without and from within — on a daily basis. I began spending an inordinate amount of time in my bedroom "studying."

"What the hell are you doing up there?" my father shouted from the stairwell.

"I'm studying art history! Leave me alone!"

The pressure of adolescent biochemistry mounted on a daily basis. On all sides there were beautiful women being menaced who needed rescuing by a brave knight, whether mail-clad or sporting army pants and a bare sweaty chest. But, I wondered, once the damsel was rescued, then what? Do we get married and move to Levittown, where she could throw Tupperware parties while the guys tied flies so they could go fly fishing—where, alone together, they could drink hard liquor and relate stories of when they were young and brave (you know, when babes were babes and there was a threat around every corner)?

The family photo album sported a picture of my father in his second lieutenant uniform while he was stationed in Panama. A photo next to it showed one of his buddies with the camp's pet python draped over his neck; the thing looked like a prize-winning sausage. Both my father and his buddy were smiling broadly. I remember hearing my father talking to his hunting buddies Dreck Bimbler and Joey Angelovich about the good times he'd had in the army in Panama, drinking rum and smoking pipes and whatever. But they never talked about rescuing damsels in distress.

It was confusing. They drank and smoked. They were in the army, but didn't rescue young women in distress. And here I was, panting to ride into battle against bloodthirsty lecherous Japanese colonels and raving cannibals to rescue swell-looking and scantily-clad girls. It was all very romantic, and all very lame. In Mauch Chunk, there were no villains to attack, no damsels to rescue.

A scenario began to form in my addled, increasingly testosterone-fueled brain. It involved the Knights of the Round Table and lances and jousting tournaments and some of the guys from the gang—and a potential audience of young damsels. But first I had to get on top of all this bubbling and broiling emotional mess. I needed some facts—about sex and girls and forbidden desires (and, of course, about anatomy).

And, honest to God, it came to me in an unexpected and very bizarre way one afternoon on the corner of Center and Third Streets on the way home from school. Jimmy Gmitter, an olive-complected classmate who was planning to go into the priesthood—and whose mother was a widow—began to tell me all he knew about the magic and mystery of sex. I was too needy and goofy to quiz him on where he'd found out all of this. (It wasn't like he had a father or anyone who could tell him stuff from the man's perspective. I'd often met his mother, and she certainly wasn't someone whose mouth would even utter the word *sex*.) But my ignorance must have been obvious because, out of the blue, as we came down Center Street and began to cut across on our way to South Street along Third — where I'd cut down South and he'd continue on Third until he crossed The Swinging Bridge — he gave me a seminar in what sex was all about.

Naturally, he couched all of it in Catholic-Church-approved philosophies and phraseology. No halter-top-wearing Nazi babes in this discussion. It was all within the Catholic context — but it was brazenly direct and graphic. It felt really odd and almost dirty that this was coming from Jimmy Gmitter, who, of all the altar boys in our class, was probably the most pious.

If you wanted a stereotype of an altar boy (a Knight of the Altar), Jimmy was it. He was fervent in his Latin prayers at the Mass, he was efficient in walking through his altar duties (never having to try twice to snuff out a candle at the end of Mass), and he was the best of all of us at kneeling with his back straight, his hands folded and his thumbs crossed, and with the prerequisite beatific expression on his face. He was the perfect altar boy — and now, strangely, my conduit for the lowdown on all things sexual.

"You must never, ever touch a girl down there," he said, pointing at my crotch. "If you do, and it's a Tuesday, Thursday, or Saturday, your fingers will vibrate and in nine months she'll have a baby and you'll have to get married and get a job."

I stopped in my tracks. "Don't you have to do something else besides touching her with your hand?" I asked, without a hint of a stutter. (My mind wasn't concentrating on speaking; it was concentrating on the mysteries of life itself.)

"No," Jimmy said emphatically. "All you have to do is touch her." He looked around as though there were sex-starved spies behind every bush and shrub. "Sometimes, if you think about having sex too hard, you can make her pregnant just like that."

This was astonishing to me, doubly so because I had turned into an avid science fiction fan, and I knew about ESP. I'd spent hours at one point trying to move an apple core across the table and into the garbage can by telekinesis. All the apple core did was turn brown.

"Come on," I said. "You can't *think* somebody pregnant."

"God did," Jimmy was quick to remind me. "Don't you believe in the Virgin Mary?"

Well, of course I did. But what does that have to do with my mind doing strange and obscene things to Ann Haggerty the next time I saw her?

We resumed our walk up the little hill in front of us. A big old black Buick drove past spewing oily smoke. I didn't know the guy driving it, but he was wearing a fedora pulled down over his eyes. Maybe he was trying to eavesdrop on Jimmy Gmitter's seminar: "The Astounding Powers of Mental Sex."

"Who told you this stuff?" I asked.

"Nobody had to tell me," he said.

Now, come on, I thought to myself. If somebody has to teach you where the Isthmus of Panama is or which is the second planet from the Sun or which branch of government interprets laws, surely somebody's got to teach you about the most important subject in the world. The Virgin Mary was one thing, but The Virgin Sexpert? Come on!

"Come on," I said out loud. "Where'd you get all this stuff — really?"

Ol' Jimmy looked at me in a very serious and accusatory way. "Are you saying I don't know anything — that I'm stupid?"

Although Jimmy wasn't on the honor roll, he certainly wasn't dumb, so I wasn't gonna call him stupid.

"I'm not saying yo-yo-you're da-da-da-dumb," I said, my mind wandering off sex and onto things much more practical. "But everybody has to learn stuff fra-fra-from sa-sa-sa-somewhere. Don't they?"

"Does somebody have to tell you the sky's blue?" he asked.

I thought about that for a second. "Ah-ah-I had to la-learn wha-wha-what *blue* was first," I said.

"Well, now you're just being a wise guy," he said. "Now I'm not gonna tell you anything else. You don't deserve to know about sex."

"Of course I do!" I affirmed.

"Well, I'm gonna tell you one more thing and then if you wanna know more, you're gonna have to pay me," he said.

Ah! So that was it — a con job. Set the hook with a few tidbits, get the mark interested, and he'd have to come back for more because he couldn't stay away from it once it got hold of him. I nodded that I'd listen to one more thing.

Jimmy almost whispered. "If you stick your tongue in a girl's ear it'll turn her on and she'll let you do anything you want."

I shivered. Stick your tongue in her ear? What if there was earwax and stuff in there? What if your tongue went in too far and hit her brain? (Our mothers always told us in order to protect the delicate bones and membranes in the ear, to never stick anything in your ear but your elbow — solid advice, then and now.)

I stood alone on the pavement. Jimmy Gmitter was walking away, on his way to his home and his over-protective mother. She, of course, had received a tongue in the ear — at some point, many years before — and had been touched "down there" on a Tuesday, Thursday, or Saturday, so that Jimmy could be born, only to grow up and spend his spare time torturing me with misinformation.

I didn't run after Jimmy Gmitter to extract more sex info from him, and he didn't look back to check on me. He continued to walk away. A few days later (probably still piqued at me for doubting his sexual bona fides), out of the blue, he told me, "Girls are never going to like you. You have a fat ass."

At the time I was almost as skinny as Aboo Hascin. If *anyone* had a fat ass . . .

For the next few weeks, we drifted apart and didn't walk home along Center Street together. But, in typical boyhood fashion, the estrangement lasted only those couple of weeks, and we picked up where we had left off — not dwelling on Jimmy's Sex Secrets. Besides, there were other things that needed doing, and Jimmy said plainly that he didn't want to have any part of it — planning for the Royal Joust.

My brother Drew was too shrewd to get involved in this harebrained operation. Besides, he was getting pretty good at talking to girls. He didn't need the wisdom and the allure of the ancient armored warriors like the rest of us thought we did.

After consulting a half-dozen of the library's picture books detailing dueling and jousting and the slaying of infidels in the days of King Arthur and King Richard, Catfish and I cooked up a plan. We would put together a jousting tournament, to which we would invite the fair damsels in our class, in order to impress them with our chivalrous qualities — toward maybe, some day, sneaking a snaky tongue down a female ear canal when the moon was full and the mood was right, and it wasn't Tuesday, Thursday, or Saturday. (We were too young to get married and have kids.)

We cleared a section of the dump behind Fish's house, where the bank was tilted gently downward, but nowhere near as steep as it was behind my house. We cleaned out the brush, moved some of the trash, and strung ropes around certain trees in order to set the boundaries of the field of battle.

Then we went shopping at the lumberyard, which was made easier by the fact that a windstorm had blown a big tree down, and it had fallen over part of the fence in the back of the yard. Little monkeys that we were, we could access the heart of the lumberyard effortlessly. We weren't going to steal anything valuable — just stuff that they usually broke up and threw away.

Our main target was the wooden spacers that were used between major-league planks. The spacers were about ten feet long and roughly two inches by two inches. They were used to keep the planks from sitting directly on top of each other, coming into contact with each other, and getting scratched. It was a happy accident that the spacers were almost exactly the size and shape as a lance. We collected a half-dozen lances and stored them in Fish's cellar.

Then we relieved a half-dozen neighborhood trash cans of their lids and added them to the stash. They'd make perfect shields and we'd return them after the tournament was over. We then made the rounds of the appliance stores, scrounging through the trash piled in the back. We found what we were looking for — boxes that had recently contained major and minor household appliances. The stores had extracted the toaster ovens and radios and small refrigerators to use as floor samples. The boxes were perfect for our needs.

It took several trips to lug the boxes down to the lair of the Gallant Knights, but, when we were done, we went to work with our pocketknives cutting out arm holes and neck holes in the larger boxes. From the smaller boxes, we sculpted elaborate helmets to protect our faces, some with vertical and some with horizontal slits across the front so we could see (sort of). We scavenged for bird feathers, which we tied together to make varicolored plumes to attach to the peaks of our helmets.

There were some discarded downspouts in the dump, and we tried to use them for our arm armor, but they were much too long. Our elbows couldn't bend inside them, and we didn't have a hacksaw to cut them down to size, so we gave up on that idea.

Paul "Pockets" Gavornik, Catfish's father, gave us a half-empty gallon of silver paint. "Just don't get it all over yourselves," he warned us. "The stuff is hell to get off skin." We never asked him what he used the other half-gallon of paint for. The only thing we could think of that we'd ever seen painted silver was, occasionally, the front of a Lehigh Valley Railroad locomotive. But there were no tracks leading to Pockets' gas station on Fourth Street.

The silver paint, of course, was perfect for painting our cardboard appliance boxes so they'd look like shining armor. We fashioned swords from picket fence slats and painted the shafts silver, too.

There was an old bedsheet that we tore apart and used crayons to paint on colors and symbols for our knightly banners. Catfish decided to use a shark as the symbol of his royal house instead of the catfish. Being named Richard, I did some research and borrowed the lion's head of Richard the Lion-Hearted.

(Years later I would get sucked in by a magazine ad and order my family's coat of arms on a set of glasses. The Benyo coat of arms was less than spectacular. On the bottom was a mound — resembling a small pile of manure — and coming out of the top of the mound was a crescent with the points upwards, and above that, a five-pointed star. Were the Benyos originally Muslim manure-gatherers?)

We toiled over those pennants longer than we did anything else, because they symbolized who we were, and they would be displayed near the tip of each lance, which we busily whittled to a point as sharp as a No.2 pencil.

When we were finished crayoning our symbols and devices, we turned the bedsheet strips over and did the other side, so our symbols could be seen from any angle. This was serious stuff. Raymond Otto wasn't very good at making a prancing horse, so I helped him by muscling out the stick legs and doing some shading to give it some depth. By the time we were done, I'm not sure whether they would have appealed to Andy Warhol or Grandma Moses — perhaps Salvador Dali. (I do think we should have received extra credit in school for all the research we did and for the realizations we reached about the difficulty of being a Knight of the Round Table — or of any other-shaped table.)

We needed help putting on our armor, and it got mighty hot in there, especially if we raised our body temperature by doing anything active — like walking or running. And we couldn't see for squat when we tried to look out through the slits in our helmets. Oh, yeah, and silver paint smelled really bad in an enclosed place coated with it. It didn't take long to get woozy. But kids are more adaptable than adults give them credit for, and through persistence and determination, we gradually increased our knightly skills.

After a particularly serious session, we were sprawled on the sward. (We were also teaching ourselves to talk the way we thought knights of that era talked.) We began to fantasize about how much better the whole enterprise would be if we had horses to ride. (One thing we *did* understand about girls was that they *loved* horses.) We went so far as to consider the idea of taking turns being horses, so that *whomsoever* was the knight at the time would look impressive mounted upon his trusty and sturdy steed. We were thinking about horses in terms of cowboy heroes' horses, though — sporting Western saddles and all — complete with lasso and rifle. (We hadn't yet read Mark Twain's *A Connecticut Yankee in King Arthur's Court.*)

At one point, we tried doing our knightly jousts while riding bicycles, but they were too unsteady. Besides that, sitting on the saddle of a bicycle tended to hike the body armor up so that the knight's head sank into his armor and he was suddenly riding blind. We had more than a few crashes trying to make that idea work. (It never did.)

We were nearly set for the big tournament. There were six of us, and we planned to take turns fighting each other one-on-one, while those not fighting at the time would assume the roles of squires and retainers and such. We had broken the duels down into several categories: sword versus sword, jousting (lance against lance), sword versus mace (a Christmas snowball made of plastic at the end of bicycle chain that was in turn attached to a hammer handle), and the grand finale — The Royal Melee, which was all six of us mixing it up with whatever weapons were at hand.

We originally planned to call the finale The Grand Mayhem, but that sounded too out of control, too chaotic. As far as the *Royal* part of the melee went, we were beginning to see that just about everything that was anything in England had to be called *royal* — as though the king and queen owned it and they were only loaning it out to the serfs to keep them occupied so they wouldn't think about revolting.

We picked a Saturday less than two weeks down the calendar as the date for this extravaganza. We were then confronted with the challenge of securing the audience of girls we were hoping for. None of us was very good at talking to girls, so obviously, walking right up to a live girl and saying, "Hey, baby! Ya wanna attend The Royal Tournament this Saturday?" was out of the question. We were afraid they'd start twittering like they did and might laugh at us — which would really deflate the fragile ego of a Gallant Knight.

In one of the picture books we'd consulted at the town library, there was a drawing of a proclamation announcing a tournament. So we decided that a proclamation was the way to go. We immediately set to making up a royal proclamation. I wish that either my memory was strong enough that I could recall exactly what we put into the proclamation or that I had a copy of it — but I don't. And that's for a very good reason as you'll see.

We slaved for hours over our elaborate proclamation, both to compose it, and then to do the printing of each poignant word.

(Remember, this was before Magic Markers and way before personal computers with 437 fonts.) We used words like *whereas* and *heretofore*, and expressions like *Hear ye, hear ye*. Since there were no Xerox machines available for our needs, the single copy we slaved over was, well, the *only* copy.

Since we were doing this behind Catfish's house, we designated him to be the document's caretaker and guardian — a big mistake.

Catfish took relatively good care of it over the next few days as we walked him through the process we planned to use to line up our audience of panting, eager, beautiful young damsels. He was to keep the proclamation flat in one of the large-format Knights of the Round Table books we'd borrowed from the library. At appropriate times at school, he was to walk around with the book and sidle up to a potential lady-in-waiting, nudge her, and open the book to reveal the proclamation. He would give her a chance to read the skillfully worded, enticing proclamation and then ask, "Will you be able to attend, M'lady?"

It seemed simple enough to all of us — but, apparently, not entirely so to Fish. On the day he was to begin the proclamation process, he didn't have the book with him and apparently didn't have the proclamation either. "Wh-wh-where is it?" I asked as we walked into class.

In what seemed a particularly defensive response, he simply said, "Don't worry. I'm takin' care of it — my way."

Well, simply put, *his* way wasn't what we'd hoped for. During the second period, I had a ringside seat to Catfish doing it *his* way.

He'd folded up the 8½-by-11-inch piece of paper until it was the size of a baseball card. When I saw that, I cringed, remembering all the work we'd put into creating it. And hey! What was he doing? He was passing it across the aisle to Ann Marie Biank! At first, she looked confused, and then angry — Fish was bothering her when she should have been coloring in Chile on the map of South America that Sister Mary Michael had passed out to the class.

Catfish's hand, with the folded proclamation at the end of it, hung out there in the middle of the aisle like a catnip ball waiting for the cat to notice it. Ann Marie shook her head to indicate that she didn't want the damned thing. There was the shuffling of papers and the scratching of colored pencils and the concentration of kids trying to keep their pencil points inside the borders of Chile.

Sister Mary Michael, in the front of the room with her back to us, walked back and forth at the blackboard, printing the major exports of Chile in big block letters. Ann Marie Biank was getting annoyed at Catfish's insistence that she take the note. But Ann Marie Biank was an intelligent young woman and a good student (an excellent speller; nearly as good as Christine Mandracia) and she didn't want to turn this into a major confrontation that would draw attention. So, in order to appease the insistent Catfish, she finally accepted the note and slid it under her map.

At that point Sister Mary Michael turned around and put out her hand. Those habits the nuns wear hide an awful lot of stuff, and obviously sewn into the habits is a peephole for a third eyeball, this one looking out the back of their heads — they miss nothing. She snapped her fingers once; Ann Marie Biank slid the note out from under her map and handed it over. Catfish looked like he was going to slug poor Ann Marie. I felt a huge dollop of sweat escape my armpit and plop into the sleeve of my white shirt.

Sister Mary Michael took the note to her desk, sat down extra slowly, and began unfolding it as though it contained a king cobra. When they had you, the nuns were really good at drawing out the misery. They were the bar-none masters of disasters. I guess they didn't have too much else to do once the day was over but think of ways to torture kids. A second dollop of sweat plopped into the other sleeve.

And still the unfolding of the proclamation continued. Cancel out the king cobra analogy. She moved like an anthropologist carefully unfolding the brittle, dry folds of a papyrus that holds the first-ever-written words of God. That image more closely approximates the patient care Sister Mary Michael was employing to get to the message of this diabolical document. The drama was palpable. The entire class was mesmerized. There was not a sound that might drown out the rustle of each little fold unfolding.

Catfish dragged a white shirtsleeve across a furrowed, sweaty brow, and he seemed to have developed a tic in his neck. They hadn't yet invented bobble-head dolls, but the first time I saw one, it reminded me of seeing the back of Catfish's head as he waited for Sister Mary Michael's guillotine to fall on it.

For my part, besides the fetid jungle juices dripping from my armpits, I was growing a nervous tic of my own, but it was inside my brain. It occurred to me that just because Catfish was now a beached flounder, it didn't mean that the rest of us were. Catfish — Gallant Knight that he had practiced how to be over the past few weeks — might snap his backbone into place and take the hit himself, leaving the rest of us out of the firestorm to come. Maybe that would happen. I'd known Catfish since we were five and he was one of my best friends. Maybe he'd protect his buddies. Maybe . . .

It had never occurred to me that putting together a knightly joust and inviting some fair maidens to come by to watch was really an OK thing. I knew there was something wrong with it. It wasn't going to be held on school grounds or on a school day, and it might even be somewhat educational. But of course no such rationalization ever crossed my mind. What crossed it was the realization that if we had to sneak notes around about this, and if there were girls involved, it must be wrong, and sinful (and Trouble — with a capital T).

And it was. And Sister Mary Michael was now doing a dramatic, drawn-out raising of her laser eyes from the crayoned proclamation, from wading through all of those "heretofore"s and "Hear Ye, Hear Ye"s, and she was zeroing in on Ann Marie Biank. "Who gave this to you?" she demanded, her voice low and menacing.

Ann Marie Biank, who never did anything wrong and never got into trouble and who was now front and center on the carpet, was struck speechless. She tentatively pointed across the aisle at Catfish.

Even from the back I could see Catfish's incredible fake look of surprise, as though this were — completely and absolutely — news to him. It said, "How could you think such a thing? I was just sitting here filling in that long tall narrow map of Chile." When Catfish got nervous, he stuttered as well as I did. "Wha-wha-what?" he muttered. Then he shook his head vigorously. If it were a cartoon, beads of sweat would have flown off him like water off a dog that comes out of a stream and shakes himself dry.

Caught up in the drama — no, stunned by it — Ann Marie forgot to retrieve her pointing finger, and it stuck out like a skeleton at a Halloween party pointing at the person who poisoned the punch. Sweat popped out on the back of Catfish's neck. He still shook his head, as though the more he shook it, the more the good nun would buy his story. But that good nun just totally ignored his pleas of innocence. "What other boys are involved in this . . . this illegal activity?"

Catfish's head was still shaking in the negative, but the words "illegal activity" had set off a charge among the other kids. The collective drop of every jaw in the room now shattered the silence. *Illegal activity!* My God, she was good. She'd managed, by the use of two words, to manipulate Catfish into a corner, stung by the eyes of every one of his classmates.

Inside each of their heads, inside each of their psyches, and inside the cache of their previous experiences in life, *illegal activity* meant something different — entirely unique and terrible — to each one of them. Each child thought of the worst possible thing they'd ever heard of or ever experienced.

Jimmy Snyder — who had a pretty good store of troubles he'd seen — had, the year before, zipped up way too fast while in "the boy's lavatory" and had gotten his nipper zipped. Would that be the first thing that came to *his* mind? Something painful and filled with the (so far) worst imaginable sex organ experience?

Ron Hydro, who would eventually become a Pennsylvania state trooper — was he thinking of some low-life crime? Some crime against all that was thought of as good and holy — like taking coins out of the poor box instead of depositing them into it? Something that would involve twenty-five to life?

They say that when you're about to die, your life is unspooled like a movie in front of your eyes. That's not the case when you're imagining your punishment for an unspeakable crime. What is unspooled in front of your eyes are the things you were planning to do later, after you got out of school, and maybe stuff you were planning to do the next weekend and now won't get to do.

But wait. What we were planning to do that coming weekend was have the Royal Joust! *Illegal activity?* How did she know that fast that we'd stolen the spacers of wood to use as lances and that we "borrowed" garbage can lids? (We were going to return those after we were done with them. Honest.)

I slyly looked around the room and noted the expressions on the faces of my fellow students. It was obvious that Jimmy Snyder was pleased that for once in his life, he wasn't at the center of The Trouble. Christine Mandracia had a look of concern on her face — a look that was generous enough to encompass everyone in the world who at that moment was in Trouble. My one true (real-world) love, Ann Haggerty, seemed a bit confused about what was going on. But in reality, she was one of the driving engines of the whole stupid unraveling Royal Joust thing. Oh, she was lovely, guilty (by association), and simultaneously clueless.

And then it happened. Catfish turned true to form. He buckled. Some vital internal organ from somewhere in the lower regions of my body broke loose and floated up to get lodged in my throat as Catfish rattled off his five accomplices. And my name led the list. I felt my face turn hot and red — busted, at twelve-years-old, *for an illegal activity.*

There was smoke building up inside Sister Mary Michael's habit. I could smell it. She stood up and delivered one of the best guilt-bomb speeches I'd ever heard.

Now, some pre-teens and teens are immune to an adult laying a guilt trip on them. They sit there and pretend the guilt trip is having some effect when, in reality, they are wearing guilt-resistant chain mail. When it comes to guilt, I'm not sure if it is born in the bone or applied later, but Jews and Catholics seem to have it perfected.

It's sort of like a rash that is heat activated. Get the red flush of embarrassment from something you did wrong, and the rash blossoms into a glorious corsage of red and pink and purple and white itchiness that no amount of scratching will satisfy.

Sister Mary Michael was in rare form. The guilt flowed like water from a knocked-over aquarium. The nuns take a special course at nun school that helps them perfect the guilt trip as an art form. Some nuns, of course, are merely adequate, while others are of the genius mold, able to turn the most innocent of occurrences into major productions — able to transform a mere slip of the tongue into a treble hook through the lip of the transgressor.

Sister Mary Michael went into Guilt Trip Number Three: Something You Haven't Yet Done But Were Going To Do That Is Very, Very Wrong And You're Going To Hell If You Don't Immediately Repent. The speech lasts approximately eight-and-a-half minutes and it's always the same. It was as if she had a set of recordings implanted in her that she could activate by pulling a little string — with a ring on the end of it — that hangs out of the side of her neck. If you've got the guilt thing down, it doesn't matter if you know damned well this is the seventeenth time you've heard Guilt Trip Number Three this semester. The rash starts to itch, you start to envision scenes of Hieronymus Bosch's Hell, and you want to die — all the time knowing (on some level) that the idea of the Royal Joust was just not sin-worthy, that there was nothing wrong with what you were going to do.

Oh, the place we made our announcement might be a bit wrong-headed. But after all, pre-teens and teens (and post-teens to about twenty-five years of age) are bound to screw things up — to not think things through as well as they might. Their brains just aren't yet fully developed. (It's as though the brain is a cake that needs to stay in the oven for a long time. But we occasionally open the oven door to see how it's doing, and we realize that the entire center of the cake is still gooey. No pre-teen or teen or early-post-teen cake is ever ready to come out of the oven. That's why we do stupid things.)

The strange thing is that since no one but the nun had seen the proclamation, only she — and a handful of us boys — knew what was on it. And as we discussed before, each student was able to take his or her worst-case scenario and apply it to the proclamation. And as I peered out from under slowly moistening eyes, I could tell by the expressions on some of my fellow students' faces that they had envisioned some extremely nasty things. I was sure that not one of them came even close to the jousting tournament of The Gallant Knights. No sirree.

The bottom line was this: After administering Guilt Trip Number Three, Sister Mary Michael said this: "If I hear that any of you went to this thing this weekend, you'll be very, very sorry you did."

Unfortunately, nobody knew what she was talking about. But they'd all be sure not to go there that coming weekend, wherever it was.

But let's get the hell out of there. Let's fast forward to the day of the Royal Joust. I wanna be out of that sixth-grade classroom where the mushy guilt was sloshing around like so much raw sewage. Ugh. Out, damned spot! Out, I say!

The field of battle lay littered with the appliances of war: a lance in the weeds just off the main tournament grounds; a nearly complete suit of cardboard armor painted silver, and laid out as though the warrior within had suddenly been vaporized; and ribbons dangling from ropes that separated the spectator area from the field of battle.

Six (lowercase) "gallant knights" sat and lounged on the sward, far enough from each other that you could imagine each was quarantined with some virulent disease — perhaps the Black Plague. There was for the longest time not a syllable of dialogue — just a palpable layer of anger, resentment, frustration, and confusion.

The tension was heightened by gurgling pre-teen biochemicals pumped into the closed system by glands working overtime. Chemicals, mixing in fierce and arcane ways, inundated the organs and especially the brains of all six. There was no morally acceptable way to relieve the tension without consigning oneself to a fiery hell, so it built up like a liter of gasoline pressed into a quart bottle.

The gallant knights, all ungallant and unseen by the rest of the world, were incredibly foul of mood. Their confusion about sexuality had started to build a wall against a world they were sure knew nothing about what they were going through. Or if it did, it had not been willing to lower itself far enough to offer an explanation or to assure them that what they were feeling was not a secret, singular curse. And their current foul outlook extended from one to the other, as though they had betrayed each other in some plot none of them understood. But, being the only six guys in the world who could appreciate what the other was going through, they were reluctant to construct a wall high enough to cut each other off.

A perfectly good Saturday — every Saturday precious to the young and the old — was leaking away like motor oil from a cracked crankcase. *Glub. Blub. Glub.* We sat, heads bowed onto knees, arms wrapped around our heads, or sprawled out, as though lounging on a beach in Southern California, waiting for the sweet waves to march in and drown us.

A truck went down South Street making lots of metallic noises as though every bushing in the whole damned thing had dried out and cracked. Someone somewhere was beating the dust out of a carpet slung over a washline. Occasionally, fragments of voices reached us from Pleasant Hill's Saturday morning chores. The little breeze that existed carried the aroma of The Shit Creek to our noses. We didn't notice — because we had grown up with it in our noses and were used to it, and because our half-baked brains were preoccupied.

The glumness revolved around two sad facts: There would be no damsels coming by to watch the joust and to be impressed. And Catfish was the one who was going to have to break the silence since he'd been the one to sell out his friends.

It was incredible to us that our parents had barely reacted to the revelation of the planned joust. "Sure, I knew about it," Catfish's mother said. "What's wrong with the kids having some fun? It's not hurting anything. At least we know where they are."

"At least we know where they are." These were words kids loved to hear their mothers say, but words we hoped were not entirely true. We wanted to be secret and mysterious — off on major earth-saving errands, taking part in a joust to impress damsels who might soon be in distress and in need of a willing knight or two.

We stole furtive glances at Catfish. It was obvious that it was up to him to break the silence. He'd ratted us out.

But we were comfortable with that on one level. It was consistent with Catfish's behavior since we'd first met him. It would be even more awkward at that moment if he *hadn't* ratted us out, because then we'd have to completely re-evaluate the meaning of Catfish and how he no longer meshed with our lives the way he always had. (Friendships depend on consistency. At least he'd been consistent.)

But Catfish wasn't ready to send out a tentative feeler to see how we were handling all this. In this, too, he was not the bravest of knights at the table.

Instead, it was Raymond Otto who broke the silence. "Ya know, we're probably not supposed to be here either," he said, then paused and threw a thoughtful glance around the jousting field. "Sister Mary Michael said nobody was supposed to come here today. What if she finds out we came here anyway?"

"How's she gonna find out?" Catfish said, throwing in his baited hook, hoping to be accepted as part of the discussion.

"*How?*" I blurted out, always the sensitive one in the group. Catfish's eyebrows arched — like sideways question marks. "*How?*" I repeated. "*You'll* tell her."

Whoa. That was not a fence-mending thing to say. And everyone knew it. It certainly didn't leave Fish much room to get back into our good graces.

Junior Reis, a true diplomat, jumped in. "No. No he won't," Junior said. "He knows better than to do that."

Catfish nodded his head, more vigorously than necessary, eager to move forward at least one baby step.

"Yeah," one of the Franko kids said. "Yeah, he knows better — maybe."

It seemed like an opening, so I took it. "Yeah, maybe," I said, taking half a step in the direction of reconciliation.

"We'd better clean this stuff up," Catfish said. And that was that. Things were back to normal.

We sluggishly moved around, zombie-like, and disassembled our jousting tournament arena, recklessly pushing our armor about — the same armor we'd worked on so carefully and lovingly. Catfish broke one of the lances over his knee. Unfortunately, it wasn't his lance. "Hey!" Junior Reis said.

"What?" Catfish replied.

"That's *my* lance."

Catfish located his lance and handed it over so that Junior could break it, which he quickly and deftly did.

We spent a full hour setting the place back to approximately what it had been before the Gallant Knights took it over — but it was way cleaner than it had been. Our swords, lances, and armor were all piled together in a heap, the garbage can lids set aside to be returned to their rightful owners.

We were no sooner finished than Mrs. Gavornik came to the edge of the bank. She was still steaming over the nun condemning our tournament. That tournament, she continued to claim, wasn't going to hurt anyone. "Come on up for lunch," she said. "All of you."

We trooped up and saw that she'd stocked up on sodas and candy and chips and kid stuff in anticipation of a crowd. Lunch?

But even fueled by the sugar and caffeine in the colas and the sugar and salt in everything else, the mood of the Gallant Knights was not elevated above third-degree glum. We did, however, hold a soft spot in our hearts for Mrs. Gavornik for her belief that we'd done nothing wrong and that our efforts should be celebrated.

Catfish later reported that his mother had bought so many party eats and drinks for the anticipated crowds that the family pretty much subsisted on party food the rest of the week. This, of course, didn't break his heart, although it did ruin whatever diet he was on that week.

Back at school on Monday, there were some inquiries about how the tournament had gone. Kids, being resourceful, had unearthed the details of the proclamation. We lied and said it was a moderate success — "But hey, we really missed you." Even some of the girls asked, and several of them said they'd have come by, but they didn't want to get into trouble with the nuns. Two of the girls even asked when we were going to do it again.

Never. Our armaments were destroyed; we were without weapons — knights without armor.

Leap forward to the end of the seventh grade, the weekend before school ended in early June. I'd spent six years mooning over

Ann Haggerty. Over those six years we'd probably exchanged two dozen words, none of it having to do with feelings, yearnings, or emotions. All of it having to do with spelling and geography and Bible history.

Cousin Dave (bound-for-the-priesthood) Herman got tired of hearing about my suffering and pining, so he cooked up a plot to get me close to Ann Haggerty. As it happened, Ann's best girlfriend, Marie Rimsky, was a third cousin of mine on my father's side. My grandmother had been a Rimsky before becoming a Benyo.

Dave made contact with Marie, who was also in our class, and learned some things I should know. Among them was that Ann Haggerty's favorite song was Paul Anka's "I'm Just a Lonely Boy." Paul Anka, that bastard — the one who was messing with my TV girlfriend, Annette Funicello. (She'd sung "Tall Paul" for Paul Anka, even though, when he appeared on *American Bandstand*, he didn't look all that tall to me.)

Now, due to having a severe stuttering problem, my concentration was often absorbed by trying to get simple words to come out of my mouth without them being broken and abused and wearing casts and hobbling on crutches. As a result, I was not the best memorizer in the world. You've heard of people who have photographic memories; I have clear-stream memories, in that I can see through them as they slide on by and disappear. But I determined to learn the lyrics to "I'm Just a Lonely Boy." (And why not? It could have been my theme song.)

It would have been a lot less onerous if the song had been done by my teenage idol, Ricky Nelson. I actually knew the lyrics to several of his songs from having listened to them so many times. And before I went to bed each night, I'd tape my lower lip down so that when I woke up the next morning it would be thicker, like Ricky's lower lip. (Yeah, yeah. I told you that brains at that age are half-baked.)

So I cut the lyrics out of one of those newsprint-paper magazines that carried the lyrics to hit songs, and I set to memorizing the damned thing. (I say "damned" because every time I began working on memorizing it, I flashed to Paul Anka planting a great big wet one on those luscious lips of dear Annette. But I persevered.)

In the meantime, Dave Herman and Marie Rimsky hatched a plan that Dave and I would come by her house around 2:00 P.M. on Sunday. Marie lived across from the church and a few houses down; Ann Haggerty lived two houses down on the same side of the street as the church.

I met Dave at Joe Brown's Store on the corner, and we strolled coolly down the street to Marie's house. She and Ann Haggerty were sitting on the steps leading up to the porch. Dave and Marie did some small talk, I nodded my head a few times, and Ann sat there smiling beautifully.

Although we were in class together every weekday, this was entirely different. I hoped none of the nuns were walking around the church grounds across the street. After the debacle of the Gallant Knights tournament the year before, seventh-grade boys and girls consorting in public in the middle of a Sunday afternoon might really set them off.

We continued to shoot the breeze about nothing. I can't remember one sentence or one topic that we covered, other than Dave lobbing the slow, outside pitch that I knew all the words to "I'm Just a Lonely Boy." Ann Haggerty smiled at that, but didn't ask me to sing it — which I could have done just fine because, like most stutterers, I don't stutter when I sing.

Eventually, I suggested that we walk up to the Olympian Drive-In between Eleventh and Twelfth Streets. We were between Fifth and Sixth, and although the walk to the dairy bar was uphill, kids in those days didn't balk at walking six blocks uphill, especially if there were sodas and ice cream at the end of the hike.

The four of us walked to the dairy bar and scanned the menu that was painted on the wall. Ann, bless her heart and her belly, ordered the most expensive items on the menu, and after pining over her for six long years, I realized in a flash that I couldn't afford Ann Haggerty. She was just too expensive for me. I'd worked eight hours the day before to earn two bucks (one of which went directly into my college fund), and here I was going through more than that on what wasn't even, strictly speaking, a date.

It wasn't that I was cheap or ungenerous; it was the realization that if I were to date Ann Haggerty, I'd be broke all the time. No more baseball cards, no more RC Colas, no more comic books, no more movies, no more records, no more books. For a kid who had, just a month earlier, turned thirteen years old, the prospect of such a limited lifestyle for the next several years was just too much.

And besides, after another year of school, Ann Haggerty and I would be going in different directions. She'd be going to Marian High and I'd be going to Jim Thorpe High, and we'd never see each other. So why get something started that had no future?

One taste of the fruit I had admired from afar for six years was enough. Aaaaarrrrrgggghhhh! Six perfectly good years badly invested. We walked back to Marie Rimsky's porch, and Dave and I walked off and that was that. My love life was kaput.

Within the next year, however, all the boys in my class would receive an even ruder awakening about girls. And that went like this:

Each year, when the eighth graders at St. Joe's graduated, they took a class trip to Dorney Park in Allentown, where they had a swell roller coaster. Well, that tradition came to an abrupt end in the spring of 1960 when the good nuns cancelled the trip. Why? Because the girls in our class were so predatory and aggressive that the nuns were afraid to let the class go to Dorney Park for fear of what might happen to the dim-witted boys when the girls got them alone in the Tunnel of Love.

Honest. They cancelled the class trip. And they weren't coy about the reason. They made it quite clear why we weren't going to Dorney Park. They were afraid there would be rapes and deflowerings — of the boys.

It was our first run-in with emerging feminism, and, I gotta admit, I wasn't too thrilled with it. What can be good about forcing you to miss your class trip?

My mother and a few other mothers of the boys in my class called the nuns to ask why the boys couldn't go on their class trip by themselves. How was it fair that they were being punished for the sins and potential sins of the girls in the class? There was also a suggestion to have the boys go one day and the girls go another day, not too unlike how the parish ran Our Lady of the Hills Summer

Camp. (Remember? The boys went one week and the girls went the following week.) But no . . . it was all or nothing.

Our class trip was gone — the first time in the history of the school. Maybe having all those first-born kids in the same class wasn't such a good idea. Maybe this whole sex thing was way over the head of the average fourteen-year-old boy. Maybe it was a plot by the nuns to get the boys pissed off enough at the girls so that all the boys would sign up to go to the seminary. Maybe things would be different in the fall when we went to high school. The high school was another six blocks beyond St. Joe's, and another dimension away from the cloistered life at St. Joe's Grade School.

Things would be different in public school: some of the same kids, but an army of new kids; teachers who didn't wear habits and rosaries; kids who didn't wear uniforms; a bigger student body; and more sports than just CYO basketball.

Yeah, sure — things would be different, better, more worldly, more girls, more of everything.

Yeah, sure.

Afterword

War is supposedly 95% boredom interrupted by 5% stark terror. Childhood is a bit like war, at least in the proportions. For 95% of the time, nothing much happens, but for 5% of the time enough happens that memory tracks are laid down which can lead to rhapsodizing about childhood while we rock in our rocking chairs on the front porch of a nursing home.

The preceding stories are snippets from that 5% of the first fourteen years of a typical kid's life — unique in that it occurred in the hard coal region of eastern Pennsylvania during its rapid and then lugubrious decline, but universal in the events and emotions kids in that era experienced.

It is theorized that we are what we are going to be by the time we are five years old, our genes spun in the cotton candy machine that is Mom and Pop getting it on — letting the two sets of genetic materials, that took eons to form, come together in whatever dominant/recessive mix is on for that day. All the remaining input is nurture (or lack of same), although I think a lot of that nurturing is shaped not just by our parents, but by siblings and friends and television, since we spend so much more time with them than we do with our parents.

Of course, there are exceptions. It is rare for a person to change in a fundamental way, for a Saul to be converted to a St. Paul on the road to Damascus. But it happens. Matt King changed his ways overnight. Drew said that Matt King now lives peacefully in the house his grandmother owned, is married, has two kids, and (for all we know) has never been incarcerated — a fate that we were all certain would be his.

I thought about changing Matt's name in these pages to protect his new hard-won innocence, but then thought better of it. He is who he is, was who he was, and never evinced any qualms about gaining notoriety.

Drew, Catfish, and I don't always come off all that well either. But then, we were all goofy kids cursed with faults and foibles — some naturally inbred, others nurturingly inflicted. In the end, I decided to name names, to throw the innocent in with the not-so-innocent, the good with the bad, the saints with the sinners.

There was also the matter of what to put into the book and what to leave out. Obviously, I had to set the background of my life by presenting some of the family members who caused it — those who had some influence on the outcome.

It may seem a bit odd to play up my grandfather, Pete Herman, as much as I did, when women played such a large part in my young life. In spite of the fact that I was raised on a block with mostly boys, my early life was dominated by women: born of Dorothy who stayed home with Drew and me, delivered and circumcised by Dr. Jane; the family dominated by two strong and scary grandmothers; we boys watched over on South Street by the House of Women, regularly beaten up by Patsy Bronko, and taught through eight grades by a corps of nuns.

Peter Herman was a refuge and a wizened mentor; we got along just swell, due in large part to my being his first grandchild — and a male at that. Pete was always supportive and never critical that I recall — not even about my stuttering.

Once the basics of birth and place were laid out in the first few stories, it became a matter of picking and choosing from among memorable incidents jotted down on a stack of three-by-five cards. I wanted to share the incidents that would feature Mauch Chunk/ Jim Thorpe and capture the lives of the kids who lived then, at the end of that long period in American society where kid-dom changed very little — a period that was on the verge of changing dramatically as the 1960s rolled in.

Would you like to hear, in synopsis form, some of the stories that didn't make the cut? Okay, here are my favorites:

Weaned by a Cathode Ray Tube

Being the birth canal of cable television, Carbon County — hemmed in by mountains but pulling in stations from Philadelphia and New York City — had a very special relation with the boob tube. I thought about devoting a full chapter to the whole phenomenon of people — who had never gone more than twenty miles from their birthplace — living vicariously through big-city television.

We used to get *The Million Dollar Movie* on WOR-TV, Channel 9 in New York, which played the same movie five nights a week, using the theme from *Gone with the Wind* as its own theme. And then there was *Double Chiller Theater* on Saturday nights, hosted by Roland (later renamed Zacherly), who, every once in a while, would insert himself into a scene of the movie he was showing. And of course, there was *American Bandstand* out of Philadelphia (before it went national), where the Catholic girls would stop off at the studio on their way home from school (still in their school uniforms) and dance to Chubby Checker.

The Phenomenal Fantastic Fart

Boys have always been fascinated by body functions. They think all such noises and smells were created for their amusement. This is probably why so much male humor centers on body functions and orifices.

Our wacky tribe of kid scientists used their bodies as chemical laboratories in an effort to formulate the ultimate fart. After much experimenting and reporting on our results, we did, indeed, discover The Big Bang. But since I felt it would be in bad taste to devote a full chapter to farting, I'm going to let the secret of the winning formula die with me. (I suppose I can give you a hint, though: It's a combination of a somewhat common drink and a fruit.)

Stairway to Hell

Is bigger always better? Not when it came to the new sliding board that seemed to appear overnight at Memorial Park, where Dave Herman and I spent summer days at day camp making vinyl wallets and plaster of paris busts of Washington and Lincoln — so many that we could have given one to each member of our class.

There was no announcement about the new sliding board going up. One day it wasn't there and the next it was. It was attached to the end of what we referred to as the "adult swings" — swings that were huge and from which you could get tremendous height and (if you were man enough) let go at the apex and sail through a lot of air. The sliding board was the tallest I've ever seen — sort of like one of those ten meter diving platforms.

It just went up and up, and up and it had very low sides, so if you were brave enough to climb to the top, there was no guarantee you wouldn't fall over the side once you started down. For days the new slide served as a rite of passage for every boy in East Mauch Chunk. Today, with the concerns over lawsuits, no such sliding board could exist.

Not All of Them Hid Out in Argentina

At the end of World War II, a small army of truly terrible Nazi officers escaped punishment at the hands of the Allies by fleeing to Argentina — there to vanish into the jungles and live out their lives in opulence. Some of them were mad scientists and sadists who worked at the death camps. We theorized that at least one of them, "Doc" Dougherty, D.D.S., jettisoned his German surname, moved to Mauch Chunk, and hung out his shingle.

He obsessively washed his hands, wore his all-white uniform with every crease perfectly vertical, and didn't believe in anesthesia. He charged $4 to drill out and fill a cavity, and $2 to pull a tooth. For a filling, he would grind out the cavity with a drill that turned at roughly 20 rpm, turned by an exposed serpentine belt that ran along the sides of articulating arms.

Years later I saw the movie *Marathon Man*, and while the rest of the audience cringed and hid their eyes when Sir Laurence Olivier — playing a mad Nazi dentist who'd extracted a fortune in gold fillings from prisoners at death camps — tortured Dustin Hoffman by drilling into his front tooth, my reaction was, "Hey, Hoffman, quit being such a baby!"

A Tale of Two Christmases

This chapter would have dealt with the stark difference between Christmas Eve at Peter Herman's and Christmas Day at our house on South Street. On Christmas Eve, the entire Herman family would gather at Peter and Mary's house, where Uncle Pudda would slip out of the festivities, and, a few minutes later, Santa would appear struggling under a huge bag filled with presents for the kids. It was quite a delightful affair — except on two occasions.

Once, when I was about eight, my Aunt Lorraine wouldn't get out of the bathroom so I could get in. I ended up wetting my pants in the hall and had to wear a pair of my Uncle Richie's baggy boxer shorts for the rest of the night.

The other was when Dorothy came up with the bright idea that I should do my chores for Peter and Mary but not get paid for them on the day I did them; Mary should keep my wages and give them to me on Christmas — an interesting, even intriguing idea. But on Christmas Eve, Mary *split* my year's wages, giving some to me — and the rest to my cousin Dave Herman and another first-born cousin, Bruce Herman. I ended up receiving one-third of a year's worth of wages (and Drew, being second-born, got nothing).

Christmas day at 118 South Street could go either way, depending on Shorty's mood. But let's not dwell on it. After all, it's Christmas.

Bolt from the Blue

During one period of my youth, I spent a lot of time with my cousin Dave Herman. We roamed the woods, conjured up projects to keep us busy, and generally dedicated a great deal of our time to messing around.

We had heard that the French ate frog legs, so we caught a frog and cooked him up to try it out. Unfortunately, we didn't think to gut it first, and we didn't put any water in the cast-iron pot we had hung over a campfire to cook it in. You can imagine the resulting feast. We did sample some of the charred flesh, and yes, it *did* (sort of) taste like chicken.

We used to construct all sorts of machines and devices in Dave's basement, while his mother, my Aunt Eleanor, washed and ironed clothes and watched soap operas. One afternoon, we were in the kitchen and she was talking on the phone when a bolt of lightning struck about twenty yards away in the backyard. Sparks shot through the phone, knocked poor Aunt Eleanor off her feet, shorted out the TV, and left a smoldering jagged gash in the lawn.

Naturally, we turned the whole experience into a science project, which we presented in class the next week, complete with an explanation of how a lightning rod is supposed to work. Unfortunately, Aunt Eleanor and Uncle Eppie wouldn't let us design a lightning rod for their house.

In all, there were more than two dozen stories that didn't make the cut. Some were easy to leave out, while others were left behind very reluctantly. Because I teased you with a hint, I'm sure I'm going to get bombarded with requests for the secret formula for the world's most formidable farts.

One question that came to mind after culling potential stories was this: After fourteen years of a life, did it merely come down to these few adventures? Well, of course it *didn't*. Much of the time in a kid's life is spent being a kid, going with the flow, ignoring the clock and the calendar. A lot of "down" time is used to build "up" who the kid is becoming.

And what of the stories that *were* used? Considering the problems some memoir writers are getting into these days for making stuff up, just how accurate are they? Here are a few comments on that question.

Accuracy of dialogue: Since none of the dialogue was recorded, all of it is recreated from memory in language that I hope is pretty close to authentic.

Accuracy of dates: Some of the dates are impeccably accurate. The story of *St. Joseph's Spirit* is accurate in large part because I still have the first two — and only — issues of the newspaper, and they are dated. Some of the other incidents are located as close to actual years as I could recall. My brother Drew helped me review the stories, and was generous in adding his memories to the incidents, as well as contacting some of the principals in order to mine their memories. Even with the two of us working on them, though, and despite collaboration with other folks, we may be off by a year in one direction or the other.

I recall vividly the battles in the cornfield, but am not certain exactly which year they took place. You can consider the dates of many of the childhood events to be close approximations. The events definitely *happened*, but exactly when is open to further corroboration — or contradiction — from those present.

In reviewing the stories, it occurred to me how many of the incidents happened without the intervention of one or more adults. We took part in very few adult-organized events, other than Little League and such. Reviewing the manuscript made me realize why Charles Schulz's *Peanuts* cartoons don't include adults; they just weren't part of the kid world. (This is why when *Peanuts* is on TV, the only "talking" you hear from adults is the sound of a muted trumpet.)

I also realized how fortunate I was to have Mauch Chunk/East Mauch Chunk to work with as a quasi-mythical location — once they were consigned to history with the arrival of Jim Thorpe. (William Faulkner had to create Yoknapatawpha County, Mississippi; Mauch Chunk was handed to us already complete.)

It's wonderful to have had that special place. Some of us think Mauch Chunk should be remembered as a legendary land where the knights of the garbage-can lid sought damsels to save — whether they wanted (or needed) to be saved or not. I think Mauch Chunk can certainly be remembered fondly by those of us who once lived there, and who will, eventually, take Mauch Chunk with us when we go.